Signs You'll See

JUST BEFORE JESUS COMES

RICK RENNER

Harrison House

Signs You'll See Just Before Jesus Comes
ISBN: 978-1-68031-224-9
Copyright © 2018 by Rick Renner
8316 E. 73rd St.
Tulsa, OK 74133

Published by Harrison House Publishers
Tulsa, OK 74145
www.harrisonhouse.com

4th Printing

Editorial Consultants: Rebecca L. Gilbert and Cynthia D. Hansen
Text Design: Lisa Simpson,
  www.SimpsonProductions.net
Cover: Debbie Pullman, Zoe Life Creative Media
  Design@ZoeLifeCreative.com, www.ZoeLifeCreative.com

DEDICATION

I dedicate this book to those who long for the coming of our Lord Jesus Christ and live with the hope of His soon return burning in your heart.

As we await the end of the age and the coming of the Lord, I urge you to keep your head lifted up, your eyes fixed on God's promises, and your heart postured to embrace the Holy Spirit's power. *Your redemption draws nigh!*

CONTENTS

ACKNOWLEDGMENTS

I wish to express my gratitude to all who participated in the researching, editing, proofreading, and footnoting of this book. Although I am the author, I wrote this book with the marvelous help of others who did their parts to help me with accuracy of details so that we could provide you, the reader, with a work that could be relied upon.

First, I want to say thanks to Becky Gilbert, who worked alongside me on this writing project and on several different drafts of this manuscript. Becky hovered over every word in this book, employing her God-given editorial skills to hone each word to its current state. Likewise, Cindy Hansen, my chief editor for many years, contributed to the editing process, and, as always, I am so thankful for her contribution. I also wish to acknowledge Beth Parker, who read every word of this manuscript and helped make sure my thoughts were correctly conveyed in its pages. And Susan Woodrow's attention to detail greatly assisted me in the proofreading of the text-designed manuscript.

Dougal Hansen was invaluable to me for his research, affirming of facts, and footnoting of the manuscript. A work such as this requires utmost scrutiny, and I knew Dougal's analytical mind would be invaluable for this project. I am deeply appreciative of his expertise. Additionally, I am indebted to Douglas Holte, MD, for reading and commenting on the medical sections that deal with plagues and sicknesses in the world today. Dr. Holte's professional eyes and mind ensured that our facts were accurate and up to date. For this, I am simply grateful. I also thank Chuck McConkey and John Roush for their technical help with the football illustrations.

I want to express a hearty thanks to Debbie Pullman for her creativity in producing a cover that conveys the very sobering and impacting message of this book. *Thank you!*

I cannot conclude these acknowledgments without recognizing the prayer support I received as I wrote (and sometimes *rewrote*) these chapters. I am grateful for the *hours* of praying by our partners, many of whom let us know they were praying for me. *Just Before Jesus Comes* was truly a labor of love on the part of so many. I am thankful to everyone, including and especially the Lord Jesus Christ, who is truly Lord over all.

PREFACE

IN RECENT YEARS, I've deeply studied what the Bible teaches about events that will occur at the end of the age. I am solidly convinced that we are living in the final days of this period. I believe we are nearing the rapture of the Church, which will result in the subsequent emergence of the seven-year Tribulation that will come upon the entire earth. If these days are indeed "upon us," it is especially vital for us to understand what the Scriptures teach about them.

Sometimes Christian leaders can be sensationalistic about their beliefs in end-time events. But scaring people with Bible prophecy should not be our goal, and it certainly was not my goal in writing this book. However, God in His great love has chosen to inform us explicitly about these days so that we can be prepared.

In the pages you are about to read, I have approached these end-time scriptures cautiously, logically, and reasonably. They are both revealing and alarming. But as we give attention to this topic, we must remember that nothing in the Bible was written to *scare* us; rather, it was written to *prepare* us. God *has been*, *is*, and *will be* utterly faithful to inform us about the things we need to know to live victoriously in this last season of this age.

There is so much information in the New Testament about end-time events that we cannot claim ignorance on this subject. The Scriptures tell us how we must respond to this moment in history. If we will be open to God's Word and to the Holy Spirit, we will be enlightened, informed, and prepared to live triumphantly in Christ in these times.

Beyond the passages dealt with in this work, there is an abundance of other verses in Paul's writings that explicitly describe the social atmosphere that will emerge and become prevalent in the very last days — and I plan to deal with those riveting verses in another book. Here, I primarily focus on Jesus' words in Matthew 24, which contain precise prophecies about signs that will become evident as we approach the end of this age. In much the same way that signs on a road point to a traveler's destination, the signs of the times are present for us to see — and they're appearing closer and closer together as we go.

I want you to know this book was written prayerfully and very studiously. In its pages, you will see what Jesus (and briefly, Peter and Paul) taught about signs we'll see **JUST BEFORE JESUS COMES.** Please open your mind and eyes to the Scriptures and ask the Holy Spirit to speak to you through what you are about to read.

And never forget, Ecclesiastes 8:4 declares that *where the word of a king is, there is power.* Let God's Word do its special, powerful work inside your heart as you read and reflect on the treasury of information contained in this book.

Rick Renner

Chapter One

Signs on a Prophetic Road

My wife and I live in a suburb of Moscow, Russia. On our daily drive into the city, we see signs along the road that have been strategically placed to confirm to travelers the destination to which they are headed and the remaining distance they must travel to reach their journey's end. The closer we get to the city, the closer together these markers appear. We know *by the signs* how far we have left to go before we cross the border into this immense city.

As we approach the end of our trip into Moscow, we can see the environment change. Instead of village homes quaintly situated in the outlying areas, we begin to see industry, multifamily housing, and high-rise buildings — and the roads become increasingly denser with traffic. At first, the transition is subtle and barely noticeable. But the nearer we get to our destination, the more obvious the changes become. As we reach the very outskirts of the big city, the changes appear almost abruptly.

When driving from the outlying areas toward Moscow, without these *signs* telling us where we're headed, we might think we're just wandering somewhere out in the country. In other words, we would know only intellectually that this huge territory was somewhere out in front of us. But because of markers we see along the way, we are able to gauge exactly where we are in our journey toward the city.

Similarly, the Bible teaches that we will see signs along a *prophetic* highway to alert us to where we are on God's calendar. Because of these markers that we see in Scripture, those who are spiritually attuned will be able to discern when we are approaching new territory. Jesus believed these end-time markers were so important that in Matthew 24, He described them in detail so we would be alerted that we are approaching our own destination of the close of the age and His imminent return.

Jesus placed great importance on His people's full awareness of the very last days. That's why He explicitly enumerated many end-time events — to help believers discern when these events were approaching and to help them navigate the road ahead. It is my intention in the pages that follow to dig deep into Jesus' words in Matthew 24 to see exactly what these prophetic signs are.

'WHAT SHALL BE THE SIGNS?'

Once when Jesus' disciples were gathered with Him, they asked Him very candidly, "…What shall be the sign of thy coming, and of the end of the world?" (Matthew 24:3).

Just like so many today, the disciples wanted to know what would be the visible "signs" along the prophetic road to let them know it was time for Christ to return and for the end of the age to come. But what were the disciples really saying when they specifically asked Jesus for the "sign," *singular*, that would indicate these things? We are going to soon find out!

People have always been intrigued with the future, regardless of their age. Children wonder what it will be like to be teenagers.

Teenagers long to be adults, daydreaming about what their older years will hold for them. Young adults and newly married couples ponder what it will be like to be senior adults, and those with foresight work hard to make sure they'll have enough finances for their retirement. Senior adults begin to focus more on truly important questions concerning their own mortality and life after death.

Regardless of our age or our station in life, the future that lies before each of us is not always certain or understandable to our minds.

Since the beginning of time, soothsayers, astrologists, and fortune-tellers have appealed to man's inner need to know what the future holds. Newspapers and magazines have horoscopes to "foretell" the future. People's inward drive to know the future motivates them to pay the asking price for the help of these professed prognosticators.

Like all human beings, the disciples questioned what the future held for them. They specifically wanted to know when the age would end and how they would know it was time for Christ to return. In Matthew 24:4, Jesus began answering their question by enumerating a list of indicators they would see to let them know where they were on the prophetic road to the end of the age.

The word "sign" used in Matthew 24:3 is translated from the very Greek word used to describe signposts that helped travelers know exactly where they were when making a journey. The same is true on our modern roads. Just as I see signs each day as I drive into the city of Moscow, the disciples wanted to know which "signs along the way" would alert them to the fact that the time of Christ's return was drawing near.

As I described at the beginning of this chapter, whenever I drive into Moscow, I see markers, or indicators, posted along the highway that let me know how close I am to my destination. I finally see a huge sign that reads, "MOSCOW." That final marker authenticates and confirms that I am no longer *approaching* this city, but that I have actually *entered* it.

This is exactly what Jesus had in mind when He said we would see signs along a prophetic road to indicate we are entering the territory of *the very end of the age* (*see* Matthew 24:4-7)!

'WINDING ROAD AHEAD — PASS WITH CARE'

Signposts on a road not only confirm the direction one is traveling and the distance remaining to his destination — but they also provide warnings to keep drivers safe along the way. For example, a sign that reads, "Animal Crossing" warns travelers that wildlife can be expected in that particular area — including in the path of traffic — and alerts drivers to move with caution as they approach that area.

Similar types of markers, whether communicated in words or symbols, include warnings such as: Narrow Bridge, Lane Ends, Intersection Ahead, Falling Rocks, Winding Road, and Pass With Care. Throughout most of the world, these warnings are almost the same in appearance — usually in the shape of a diamond or triangle — so that they are plainly visible and recognizable to all travelers.

Likewise, when Jesus warned us of events that will occur at the end of the age, He verbalized them in such a way that those times would be easily recognizable, not obscured or difficult to understand. Jesus gave us concrete markers to let us know where we are on our journey, approximately how close we are to our destination, and what we need to know so we can remain safe and effective on the path.

Although the Scriptures forecast that the times ahead will be fraught with difficulty, the warnings Christ revealed were intended to direct and instruct us, not send us "running for the hills"! As we lock our trust onto Him, we can be sure that He will enable us to safely navigate the road ahead of us and *pass with care* the dangers that would ensnare us or hinder our journey.

A COMPILATION OF END-TIME SIGNS

Jesus gave specific predictors in Matthew, Mark, and Luke to let us know that we are leading up to the closure of this era. By reading these three gospels and comparing what Christ said in each of them, we can assemble a list of things He said we would see as we approach the territory of the *very last* of the last days.

The following is a summary of the precursors Christ enumerated so clearly in Matthew 24:4-14; Mark 13:5-13; and Luke 21:8-19. According to these three gospels, all of the following are events or conditions that will escalate in the last days of the age. Of course, these things have been occurring *throughout the ages*— but Jesus forecasted that these particular signs would *escalate in intensity* as we approached the very end of the age.

Jesus prophesied that just before the final wrap-up of this age, we would see:

- widespread deception
- signs in the heavens
- economic instability
- great seismic activity
- legal prosecution of Christians
- warring political systems

- famines
- wars
- persecution
- pestilences
- commotions
- ethnic conflicts

- imprisonment of believers
- emergence of false prophets
- the love of many waxing cold
- fearful sights
- unknown diseases
- rumors of wars

I feel the need to state that Jesus did not list these foreshadowings to *scare* us, but to *prepare* those of us who would be living in the wrap-up of the age. His intention was that we would be able to victoriously withstand the storms that are gathering in the times directly ahead.

THE JOURNEY FORWARD

It is my conviction that we are living in the last moments of this present age. We have the keen ability to see and understand end-time scriptures more clearly because *we are living in their fulfillment!* We are surrounded with mounting evidence of what Jesus forecasted so long ago. Because of where we are on the prophetic timeline, we are seeing and experiencing up-front what other generations could only see from a distance.

These signs have the potential to either trouble our hearts or ignite our faith. Personally, my faith is *ignited* to think that God has chosen me to live in these very last days that have been long foretold in Scripture! With the equipping power of the Word of God and the Holy Spirit, we are going to see God move mightily as the last days of this age come to a close!

As we advance toward the golden moment of His return, Jesus said that we would see signs on the prophetic road to let us know where we are in time. But He

These signs have the potential to either trouble our hearts or ignite our faith. Personally, my faith is ignited to think that God has chosen me to live in these very last days that have been long foretold in Scripture!

also warned us that no one but the Father would know the exact moment when He would return (*see* Matthew 24:36). Those who have tried to fix dates on Christ's coming have embarrassingly learned that no one is able to pinpoint the exact day or hour of the Lord's return.

This book was written to be an instrument to help open your eyes to what is happening now and what will occur as we move forward in time. It is my prayer that truth from Scripture will be opened to you in a way that increases your understanding of what lies before us. I trust that what you are about to read will ignite your own faith and motivate you as never before to seek God's face.

Think About It

1. Have you noticed any changes in the "environment" of your society or culture from just a decade ago? If so, did these developments appear abruptly or did they happen over time? These changes are what Jesus referred to as "signs of the times." Think about some of the signs you've observed, as well as your biblical response to those developments.

2. If you were to write out a plan for navigating a perilous, last-days landscape, would your priority include drawing closer to Jesus than ever before — or plotting your course to "head for the hills"? Would your plan perhaps need to include changing your lifestyle or the company you keep as you prepare your heart for His return?

Chapter Two

What Is the 'End of the World' — and Where Are We in Time?

Throughout modern history, many have weighed in on what they imagined end-time events would look like — from Hollywood and its apocalyptic renderings on the big screen to science-fiction fans, psychics, philosophers, professors, and, of course, ministers and clergy.

Some of the portrayals and predictions we've seen and heard have been interesting and worth pondering biblically. Others were spectacular and riveting — worth every bit of the price of admission to the theater, where we could vicariously live in the chaotic aftermath of destruction and near-annihilation.

As a minister of the Gospel, I must weigh in on this subject by bringing you to the Scriptures and digging deeply into what God Himself has said about the "end of the world." You will see that every era throughout human history has had a documented beginning and end, and the period in which we live is no different. It had an official beginning, and it will have an official close.

So then, when did the "last days" officially begin and when will they officially end?

Nearly 2,000 years ago, amidst the political and social turmoil of their day, Jesus' disciples had similar questions in their own hearts. They specifically asked the Lord, "…What shall be the sign of thy coming, and of the end of the world?" (Matthew 24:3).

But first, there are two other questions we need to ask at the very outset in this search for answers: What does the phrase "end of the world" in this verse mean? Will the world really *end*?

The phrase "end of the world" in this verse doesn't refer to the termination of the *world*. The word "world" here is translated from the Greek word *aionos*, which refers to *an age*. Thus, the disciples were actually interested in knowing when *this present age* would come to a close. The disciples knew that this age — the one we're living in right now — would eventually run its course. So they were asking Jesus to concretely tell them how to determine when the final close to the *age* was about to occur.

The *New King James Version* states Matthew 24:3 correctly: "…What will be the sign of Your coming, and of the end of the *age*?" In Greek, the word "end" describes *a completion, conclusion, closure, culmination, a finish,* or *a wrap-up.* This emphatically tells us that the disciples wanted to know what signs would be visible to authenticate that this current period of time was experiencing its ultimate wrap-up.

The questions the disciples asked Jesus are almost exactly the same questions people are asking today. Many have an inner awareness that planet Earth is on the precipice of something tumultuous. And they are rightfully asking about the signs we'll see *just before Jesus comes.*

THE BEGINNING OF SORROWS

In Matthew 24:4-7, Jesus catalogued a list of signs that would confirm the end of the age and His return was at hand. These signs are occurrences Jesus said would happen with greater frequency and intensity as we approach nearer and nearer to the wrap-up of the last days.

Then in Matthew 24:8, Jesus stated that all of these types of events would signify *the beginning of sorrows*. What did Jesus mean by using this word "sorrows" to describe this final slot of time?

The word "sorrows" in Matthew 24:8 is translated from the very same Greek word that is used to describe the contractions a pregnant woman experiences as the time of her delivery draws near. Although there are exceptions, it is generally true that in the beginning stages of labor, a woman's contractions are spaced sporadically apart. Those early labor pains unpredictably come and go with irregularity. But as she comes closer to her moment of delivery, those contractions occur more frequently and with greater regularity and intensity as her body prepares for the task of bringing a baby into the world.

Jesus used this phrase "the beginning of sorrows" to tell us that as this period entered its last phases, the signs He was about to enumerate would occur irregularly at first. But by using the word "sorrows" — the very Greek word for a woman in travail — Christ was telling us that when the moment of His return and the conclusion of the age is *right upon us*, these signs will occur with greater regularity and intensity, almost like a woman in the pains of childbirth. Finally, when it seems the pace and pain of these events can grow no worse, this period will end, Christ will come, and a new prophetic time period will be birthed.

According to Jesus, these last-days "contractions" will begin slowly at first, just like the early stages of labor for a pregnant woman.

Then these events will occur closer and closer together — like *birth pains* — until they will seem like they're happening rapid-fire, one after another.

As you will see in the pages that follow, these "sorrows" will be felt in the earth's atmosphere, in the physical structure of the earth, in politics, in world events, and in society at large, especially as this age wraps up in its final moments.

Finally, when it seems the pace and pain of these events can grow no worse, this period will end, Christ will come, and a new prophetic time period will be birthed.

Jesus stated that no one but the Father knows the exact day or hour when Christ will return (*see* Matthew 24:36). But Jesus said it's possible for us to know when we're *approaching* the outer boundaries of the age by looking at the *signs* (*see* Matthew 24:4-7). There are many such indicators to alert us that we have already entered the territory of the closing of this period in history. And we will see many more signs or events that will occur in the years, months, and even days leading up to Christ's return for His Church.

One of the ministries of the Holy Spirit is to show us things to come so we'll know what to expect as we move forward in time (*see* John 16:13). Armed with knowledge, we can protect ourselves, our families, and our loved ones from the destructive trends that will be associated with the closing days. And we can resolve to stand strong and do the will of God, shining as lights in the darkness that will certainly increase just before Jesus returns.

MY POSITION ON THE RAPTURE

I firmly believe that there will be a split second in time when the Body of Christ on the earth will be supernaturally "caught up" to meet the Lord in the air. This is what is commonly referred to as *the Rapture*. At the precise moment when that event occurs, the door to this present era will be closed. (*See* 1 Thessalonians 4:15-17; 2 Thessalonians 2:6-8.) After the Rapture occurs, a time of intense agony — called the Tribulation — will rage across the planet until Christ *physically* returns with "ten thousands of His saints" to establish His millennial reign (*see* Jude 14).

I have studied every theological position on this topic of the Rapture, and I want to say that I respect those who have come to a theological conclusion different from my own. My belief in the Rapture is the result of nearly 40 years of simmering and percolating through countless hours of study and prayer concerning this subject.

I am convinced of these truths. However, I am also convinced that conditions *before* the Rapture could potentially become so bleak that it may very well *feel* like we've already entered the Tribulation before that time period has actually begun.

We are living in tumultuous, dangerous times. Many areas of the world are embroiled in bloody, longstanding conflicts that are being fueled by a seemingly inexhaustible current of hatred, economic instability, poverty, and desperation on all fronts. And society continues to slide further into immorality as people chase hedonistic thrills and godless lifestyles as substitutes for truth, meaning, and purpose in life. While this degradation increases, Christians who are standing by their beliefs in God's moral absolutes are finding themselves increasingly marginalized and penalized for their faith.

Based on Bible prophecy, we know that there will be a continuing escalation of these trends. As the moral descent continues, it is likely that the tide will increasingly turn against Christians who have resolved to stand by the absolute principles contained in God's Word. But these believers will be His glorious ones, through whom the Spirit of God will arise in power to bring many to repentance and faith in Jesus Christ before it is too late.

MORE SHIFTING DEVELOPMENTS

Most of us already sense the shifting and changing that is occurring in the world today — and that unsettling impression is producing a heightened sense of urgency concerning the time in which we live. Most committed Christians who know and believe the Bible are certain about where the signs are leading us. Many are seeking God with unprecedented fervor for His intervention in the affairs of man — for His purposes to be wrought in this generation and His plans to be consummated on the earth.

Just as the disciples wanted to know when the age was going to close, believers today want to know what the signs are that will pinpoint this culmination and the Lord's imminent return. There's no question that Jesus *will* return, and we have never been closer to that moment than we are right now!

The Holy Spirit wants us to know about the signs on the prophetic road that we'll see as we enter this new territory of the wrap-up of the age. He wants us to know the signs to *prepare* us for the times ahead. This knowledge is power — our ignorance is *not* bliss!

THE END-TIMES CLOCK IS TICKING

"Four hundred and fifty feet long, seventy-five feet wide, forty-five feet high. Build it with cypress; waterproof it with tar. Construct decks and stalls, and make the door wide. Build the deck three stories high, and be sure to leave an opening below the roof — eighteen inches high — all the way around the boat. Do it just like this, and begin now. A FLOOD is coming."

The plot seemed outlandish, bordering on the ridiculous for most who heard it. In fact, any thinking person hearing it for the first time might dismiss the plan as pure fantasy — *except* for the fact that it was orchestrated by God. He said it, and it happened exactly the way it was recorded, down to the minutest detail.

I paraphrased Genesis 6:14-17 (*NLT*) to make the serious point that God is intricately involved in the affairs of man on the earth — from the time of Creation to the days of Noah and to this present day. He says what He will do, speaking the end from the beginning, and then He does it — on no one else's timetable but His own (*see* Isaiah 46:4,10). The Lord spoke to Noah about a forthcoming flood years before that cataclysmic event took place. But as surely as God said it, those floodwaters came, and eight human beings were delivered — carried to safety by a heeded warning and an obedient response to His call to action.

Throughout the many years it took Noah to build the ark according to specifications, the rest of the world no doubt mocked the servant of God as he worked relentlessly to prepare for the certain days ahead. Perhaps they said to Noah, "You've been talking about this event for *years*, but it hasn't happened! Where is this 'flood' you speak of?"

Concerning the promise of Christ's return for His Church, the apostle Peter wrote that this very mindset would be prevalent again in the climax of the age. Second Peter 3:3,4 (*NLT*) says, "...In the last days scoffers will come, mocking the truth and following their own desires. They will say, 'What happened to the promise that Jesus is coming again?'..."

Peter prophesied that at this climax of the age, there will be scoffers who will mock the prophetic declaration of Christ's return. They will complain, "They've been saying these are the last days for the past *2,000 years*, but Jesus hasn't come back yet! Where is the fulfillment of this promise?"

If you ever hear someone make this remark, you should congratulate that person for his scriptural accuracy — because the past approximate 2,000 years is *precisely* the period termed by the Bible as *the last days*!

> Peter announced that the last days were officially initiated when the Holy Spirit was poured out. So for the past approximate 2,000 years, we have been living in these last days on God's prophetic calendar.

In biblical terms, "the last days" began on the Day of Pentecost. Peter announced that the last days were officially *initiated* when the Holy Spirit was poured out (*see* Acts 2:17,18). So for the past approximate 2,000 years, we have been living in these last days on God's prophetic calendar.

But in Matthew 24, Jesus was referring to the *final* time frame of this last-days period that would alert us to the fact we were entering the territory of the *very ultimate* end of the age.

Can you hear the end-times clock ticking?

A 'TWO-MINUTE WARNING' IN TIME

Let me use the example of a football game to illustrate what I mean by "*final* time frame" and "*very ultimate* end of the age." When the players return to the field just after halftime, play begins in the second half, or the *last half*, of the game. That would be an example of the *beginning* of the end. But when the game is winding down in the last half to the last *minutes* and *seconds* of the fourth quarter — that very vividly describes a *wrap-up*, or the *very ultimate* end of the game.

This perfectly depicts where we are in history. We've been playing this last-days game for about 2,000 years. But now it's the fourth quarter, and the contest is winding down to the last "minutes and seconds" before Jesus comes and the game is wrapped up.

I find it interesting that at the final two-minute warning in professional football, the game clock is stopped briefly as an official "announcement" that the concluding moments of the game are at hand. An ultimate outcome is about to be realized, and the way each team manages the time remaining on the clock can be crucial in determining which team leaves the field victoriously — and which one goes home in defeat.

> We've been playing this last-days game for about 2,000 years. But now it's the fourth quarter, and the contest is winding down to the last "minutes and seconds" before Jesus comes and the game is wrapped up.

That final two-minute warning provides an opportunity for the losing team to mount a comeback — and the winning team to clinch the victory. Each team positions itself to execute two-minute drills — strategic, last-minute maneuvers — to outwit the opponent and either score points or "run out the clock" to prevent the other team from scoring.

The two-minute warning is often used to institute a new strategy, or modify an old one, that the opponent has never seen before. Substitutions can also be made during this critical phase of the game to ensure that players' strengths are maximized to exploit the weaknesses of their opponents. Each player must understand his assignment and be ready to execute with prowess what he has been asked to do for his team.

It's also interesting that before a team ever executes one of these two-minute drills in a game, they practice that maneuver over and over, even during the team's preseason. The players prepare themselves well in advance of a game to handle the intense situations they will no doubt face in a real contest. Then on game day, when the time on the clock runs out and the final whistle blows, the agonizing preparation and sacrifice — the sweat, bruises, aches, pains, and even the injuries — all fade from memory as the final score flashes that a winner has emerged.

OUR OWN 'TWO-MINUTE WARNING' AND CALL TO ACTION

Could this "two-minute warning" be where we are now before the conclusion of this period? If so, each one of us should carefully evaluate how we are using our time. Are we doing all we can to live for Jesus? Are we studying His Word, fellowshipping with Him in prayer, encouraging believers, winning the lost, and yearning for His appearing?

Regardless of where we think we are in time, we know we're in a conflict with dark spiritual forces that seek to weaken the Church and stop its effectiveness in the earth. But those who are familiar with Scripture and have read the "back of the book" know that *Christ wins!*

If we want to participate with God in an end-times demonstration of His power, we *must* heed His "two-minute warning" concerning where we are in time and pay attention to the signs. It is absolutely necessary that we focus our attention on what the Holy Spirit is proclaiming through Scripture about the last days just before Jesus comes.

Before the clock stops and time runs out on this present age, we as believers are to remain vitally connected to Jesus and refuse to compromise. We're called to strengthen the weak, mend the broken, heal the sick, and win the lost for whom Christ died. Then we will gloriously meet the Lord in the air (*see* 1 Thessalonians 4:15-17).

As we head toward the outermost edge of the last days, you and I are on this end-times team as members of the Body of Christ. God, who summons each generation to take their part in enforcing His plan, has called you and me for such a time as this (*see* Isaiah 41:4; Esther 4:14).

A divine role has been assigned to each one of us. It has never been more important to discover that role, get in our place, and apply ourselves to it spirit, soul, and body with all the spiritual strength and enthusiasm we can receive through God's grace.

We must be fully engaged in this spiritual contest and not allow ourselves to become sidelined or relegated to "sitting the bench" in these last moments of the period. As we honor the transforming Cross of Christ and His Word, seek to get into our God-ordained places, and submit to the God-given spiritual leaders who are over us, we position ourselves to participate in this last, greatest move of His Spirit the world has ever seen.

Those who have prepared will find themselves "in their element" — doing what they do best when the heat is on at the culmination of this period. Having submitted themselves to God in difficult seasons and yielded the fruit of His Word, they will arise in the power of His Spirit with the confident knowledge they were born for this hour — for such a time as this!

A FINAL THOUGHT
ABOUT THE TWO-MINUTE WARNING

Let me share one last word about the two-minute warning in football. The history of this warning began in the early days of the sport before there were actual scoreboards that showed the number of minutes and seconds left in each half of the game. Without the sound of the two-minute warning, neither the players and coaches nor the fans knew exactly where they were relative to the end of the game.

In other words, the final two-minute warning was an authenticating *sign*, signaling to both sides that the finish of the game was near. Both teams knew at the sound of that warning that a speeding up of the game was about to occur.

There are occasions when more plays are executed in this two-minute period than in the entire previous quarter! The activity that occurs on the field during this time is usually the most exciting part of the contest. Generally speaking, everyone — from the players on the field to those watching from the stadium — is more keen and alert in this *last of the last* part of the game.

I'm not stretching the point to say that this is where the Church is today — and it's where we are headed as the clock winds down toward the end of this period. Activity in the spiritual realm is increasing in the final "minutes and seconds" on the clock — and God is calling each one of us to remain alert and ready to take our places on the field at a moment's notice.

In our final "minutes and seconds," spiritual activity will increase and opposition will fight harder than ever. It is imperative that we are keen and more alert than ever before!

Can you hear Christ warning us that this end-times "game" is speeding toward a close?

LET NOT YOUR HEART BE TROUBLED!

We live in a remarkable time — certainly a time like none other behind us. We are living in the very final "minutes and seconds" of this present era, and we are gearing up for the climax of the greatest spiritual contest of the ages: *evil versus good — darkness versus light.*

Of course, we know that Jesus Christ is the winner over darkness and evil!

The challenge between darkness and light will occur as a last-days remnant of believers push past obstacles to fulfill God's will in the earth. Equipped by the Word and by the Holy Spirit, this Spirit-empowered body of believers will declare Christ's message and fulfill His commission to win souls, disciple believers, heal the sick, and deliver those who are bound. For this faithful remnant, this is their greatest hour to shine!

But when taking stock of the issues facing the world today, from time to time you may be tempted to be stressed or anxious. Remember that God didn't give you a spirit of fear, "…but of power, and of love, and of a sound mind" (2 Timothy 1:7). *Living in fear is not God's plan for your life,* and it is not the right response to the challenges that lie before us.

Living in fear is not God's plan for your life, and it is not the right response to the challenges that lie before us.

Never forget that God chose you for such a time as this!

Amidst these turbulent times, my mind goes to Romans 8:37, which states, "…In all these things we are more than conquerors through him that loved us."

The apostle Paul penned these words during a dark, difficult season in which the Early Church faced formidable suffering and persecution. In the midst of that difficult moment, Paul took the opportunity to remind these believers that they were "more than conquerors" through Christ, regardless of what was happening in the world around them.

We're about to delve deeply into the signs that Christ enumerated in Matthew, Mark and Luke to let us know where we are in time. But first let's ponder the powerful, victorious truths in Romans 8:37 for a moment and draw all the strength we can from them. This verse must be a foundation for our lives in these uncertain times. It is essential for us to understand exactly what Paul was declaring when he emphatically stated, "…We are *more than conquerors* through him that loved us"!

The phrase "more than conquerors" comes from the Greek word *hupernikos*, a compound of the Greek words *huper* and *nikos*. By joining these two words, Paul was making a tremendous, power-filled statement. The words "more than" were taken from the word *huper*. It literally means *over, above,* and *beyond.* It carries the idea of *superiority* — something that is *utmost, paramount, foremost, first-rate, first-class, top-notch; greater, higher, better than, superior to, unsurpassed, unequaled, "more than a match for,"* and *unrivaled by any person or thing.*

Paul used this Greek word *huper* to denote exactly *what kind* of conquerors we are in Christ because of the Holy Spirit's indwelling presence in our lives. The word *huper* dramatizes our victory. It emphatically tells us that:

- We are greater, higher, better, and superior conquerors!

- We are utmost, paramount, top-notch, unsurpassed, unequaled, and unrivaled conquerors!

- *We are more than a match for any foe!*

The word "conqueror" in Romans 8:37 is the Greek word *nikos.* It describes an *overcomer,* a *conqueror,* a *champion,* a *victor,* or a *master.* But Paul joined the words *huper* and *nikos* to make his point even stronger. He was telling us that in Christ Jesus, we are *unrivaled overcomers*, *unsurpassed conquerors*, and *paramount victors*!

This word *nikos* is so power-packed that it could actually be translated as *a walloping, conquering force*!

As we move closer to the edge of this period, it may seem that so much around us is changing and spinning out of control. In the midst of the turmoil and uncertainty of the times, it is vital that we look deep inside and grab hold of the Spirit's mighty power that resides within us. We must never forget: No matter what the world tries to throw against us, how ferociously we are harassed and attacked for our faith, or how intensely society is changing all around us, God's power remains unchanged, and it equips us to be a *walloping, conquering force*!

We are *more than a match for* anything we'll face in these last days! With the Word of God in our hearts — and the Holy Spirit's power working in us — we are supernaturally equipped for any circumstance that tries to rise against us. We may face situations we've never faced before, and we may need wisdom unlike any wisdom we've ever needed. But if we will rely on the Word of God and the Spirit of God, we will have everything we need to triumph in Christ (*see* 2 Corinthians 2:14).

> No matter what the world tries to throw against us, how ferociously we are harassed and attacked for our faith, or how intensely society is changing all around us, God's power remains unchanged, and it equips us to be a *walloping, conquering force*!

We are not to be panicked or alarmed by the events that surround us — or by the signs that indicate we are nearing the end of the last days. Jesus told us about all these things in advance so we would be prepared and spiritually equipped to overcome the changes that will occur in society.

If we'll surrender to Christ in these closing hours, He will strengthen us to stand boldly for Him — and by His grace, we will experience His "walloping force" of victory in every area of our lives. We'll discover that we are more than a match for the season in which we live, and we'll end this age as shining examples of His power and grace!

Think About It

1. What consideration have you given to the end of this age and to the beginning of the next era on God's divine time-table? Have you pondered why Jesus so earnestly wanted His people to understand the times they were living in? Do you think a believer's lifestyle in this age holds any relevance to the next period on God's heavenly calendar? Why or why not?

2. Think about the analogy of a woman in labor and the contractions she experiences as the time of birth draws near. Do you sense that your generation is on the precipice of something brand new and never experienced before? If yes, how would you describe this season of preparation and expectation?

3. Compare this current season with Noah's day as he prepared for what was to come. Have you personally experienced the scoffing of "naysayers" who mock Christ's return as either a fairytale or some far-off event that seems unreal? In your own life, have you become numb in your heart to the prophecies concerning His return?

Chapter Three

The First Sign: Spiritual Deception

As we have seen, Jesus told His disciples that there would be signs along a prophetic road that would verify where we are in time as we approach the end of the age and His next coming.

Jesus listed *many* signs that would indicate we were on the road to the end, but the *very first* sign He spoke to the disciples about contained a clear warning about wide-scale, worldwide deception that would emerge at the very end of this era. Jesus warned the disciples, *and us*, of the need to guard against that deception.

In Matthew 24:4, Jesus said, "...Take heed that no man deceive you." As Jesus began His discourse on the many end-time signs to watch for, He listed deception *first and foremost* as a primary indicator that the conclusion of the age was upon us.

Before we go any further, let's see why Jesus placed such emphasis on this sign, even above other specific signs of the times.

Jesus warned believers that they must "take heed" to guard against the deception that would characterize the end of the period (*see* Matthew 24:4). The words "take heed" were intended to *jar* and *jolt* listeners to get their attention. As Jesus spoke the words "take heed," there is no doubt that the disciples perked up to *really listen* to what He was telling them. When He had their full attention, Jesus warned them that as the present age comes to a close, an end-times deception would attempt to infiltrate every part of society across the world.

The word "deceive" used in Matthew 24:4 is translated from a Greek word that means *to wander off course*. It could depict an individual who has wandered off course, or it could even describe a whole nation and even vast numbers of nations that have veered off course from a moral position they once held to be true. It suggests a moral wandering on a worldwide scale at the close of this period.

Let me try to help you more fully comprehend how this word "deceive" would have been used in Jesus' time. In the Greek, this word depicts the behavior of someone who once walked on a solid path, but who is now drifting and teetering on the edge of a treacherous route. This person has either already departed from his once-solid path and has lost his bearings as a result, or he is in the process of departing from it. The word "deceive" means he is going cross-grain against all that was once a part of his core belief system. Sadly, he is now deviating from his former solid moral position to a course that is unreliable, unpredictable, and even dangerous.

This word "deceive" tells us that there will be a mass divergence from time-tested biblical standards. By using this word in Matthew 24:4, Jesus was foretelling that a moment was coming when society would move away from the long-affirmed laws of Scripture. Although He specified *many* signs to indicate the conclusion of the age, Christ declared that this mass divergence from truth — and worldwide moral wandering — would be the *first, foremost*, and *primary* sign to alert us that the end was near. That is precisely why He named it first in His list of signs that would authenticate we have entered the wrap-up of the age.

The words of Matthew 24:4 are intended to let us know that those who live at the very end of the age will see *moral confusion* in society as deception attempts to engulf humanity with misinformation about what is morally right and wrong. I think you can see that Matthew 24:4 aptly describes what Christians are witnessing in contemporary history.

It is simply a fact that we are watching moral confusion rage among the civilized nations of the world as never before in our lifetimes. This confusion is perhaps no clearer anywhere than in the debate over gender identity — a manifestation of confusion so severe that it stuns most thinking minds. The culture most of us knew as we were growing up was established on Judeo-Christian values. But now, as the winds of change are blowing, we are watching as the world is rapidly departing from time-tested beliefs and traditions that are based on these biblical values.

The spirit of this world is working furiously to eliminate all remnants of a godly foundation from society and to replace it with a last-days deception that will ultimately usher in a time when the antichrist rules a lost world for a temporary period of time.

As a result of this near abandonment of truth and throwing away of moral foundations, confusion abounds and society is teetering on a treacherous path — just as Jesus prophesied in Matthew 24:4. The spirit of this world is working furiously to eliminate all remnants of a godly foundation from society and to replace it with a last-days deception that will ultimately usher in a time when the antichrist rules a lost world for a temporary period of time.

The fact that you are reading this book probably means you are spiritually sensitive to what is happening in the world today. So you know well that there is an onslaught of deception attacking our culture from every direction. There is a new propensity to rationalize away truth and replace it with politically "progressive" thinking. And unfortunately, like a sickness invades and sickens the human body, this end-times deception is seeping into every part of society. This "new" mindset can be found in our schools, our government, on television — and in virtually all forms of art and media.

We are living in the day the prophet Isaiah warned about when he said, "Woe to those who call evil good, and good evil; who substitute darkness for light and light for darkness…" (Isaiah 5:20 *NAS*). We who believe the Bible understood that such a time would eventually come, but we're experiencing the stark reality that it is happening right now, in our own lifetime. It's almost as if a tsunami is sweeping over our culture, attempting to eradicate all evidence of a spiritual and moral framework. As Isaiah forewarned, what was once viewed as morally wrong has become acceptable and even celebrated. At the same time, what was once upheld as the moral standard has become ridiculed as symbols of injustice and intolerance.

But all is not lost! The prophet Joel prophesied that in the last days, the Lord would visit people of all ages in a mighty outpouring of the Holy Spirit (*see* Joel 2:28,29; Acts 2:17,18). Since we are living in this time frame that is called the *last days*, we qualify for this great spiritual outpouring upon the Church!

Although there are disturbing signs of deception emerging all around us, this is not a time to despair. This is our moment to yield to the Holy Spirit and to stand strong on God's Word. If we abide in the promises of God and stand for truth, we will experience a supernatural protection against this mass deception that Jesus prophesied would arise at the conclusion of time just before He returned. God's intention is for the Church to remain *vibrant* and *victorious* until Christ's glorious appearing.

A CONFIRMED PRECURSOR
TO CHRIST'S RETURN

Under the inspiration of the Holy Spirit, the apostle Paul also prophesied that a mass deception would occur at the end of the period as a precursor to Christ's return. In Second Thessalonians 2:11, Paul specifically stated that at the conclusion of this period, a vast percentage of the population of the world would be controlled by "delusion."

In this verse in Second Thessalonians, the Holy Spirit prophesied that a last-days society worldwide will become *beguiled*, *seduced*, and *duped*. All of these words are contained in this word "delusion." This prophesied period of deception will be so intense that people will believe what is false over what is obviously true, even denying facts and truths that are common sense and that nature itself teaches (*see* Romans 1:20).

According to Scripture, this period of worldwide deception will occur at the "outer rim" of the era — marking a time when delusion will attempt to pervade every realm of society.

This agrees with what Jesus foretold in Matthew 24:4. According to Christ — and later confirmed by the apostle Paul — a mass departure from truth and an emergence of moral confusion and societal deception is one of the most important signs to let us know that the end of the age and Christ's return is upon us.

MANY SHALL SAY, 'I AM CHRIST'

Jesus elaborated on this deception in the next verse in Matthew 24, stating that before He returned, "...*Many* shall come in my name, saying, I am Christ; and shall deceive *many*" (v. 5).

The word "many" in both places in this verse is translated from the Greek word *polloi*. There is no mistaking that *polloi* refers to *large multitudes*. This apprises us that in the years leading up to the very last of the last days, large multitudes of people will be led into spiritual error on many different levels.

I once assumed that these leaders Jesus referred to in Matthew 24:5 — who declared themselves to "be Christ" — would be "guru" types appearing on the scene and claiming to have a messianic calling. Certainly there have been many over the past 2,000 years who have claimed to be *a* messiah or even *the* Messiah. The Greek does use a definite article in front of the word Christ, which would seem to point to a concrete individual who will claim to be Messiah.

However, when you consider the entirety of the verse in the Greek, the language used seems to imply that Jesus was referring to a time when a large number of spiritual leaders would go astray in the very last hours of time. In this verse, Jesus said many would come "in my name." The words "in my name" can actually mean *on the strength and reputation of my name*. Was Jesus prophesying about deceived Christian leaders who have wandered from a solid biblical path and have deviated to a path of deception?

The apostle Paul clearly stated this development would occur when he wrote about a "departure" from the faith that will occur at the conclusion of the period. In First Timothy 4:1, he wrote, "Now the Spirit speaketh expressly, that in the latter times some shall depart from the faith, giving heed to seducing spirits, and doctrines of devils...."

The Holy Spirit explicitly said that this phenomenon would occur at the very last of the last days — and that it would take place inside the Church as some "depart from the faith." Herein, the Spirit sounded a clear warning: We must be aware that in the very last days — just before Jesus comes — some inside the Church will slowly *depart* from the sound teaching of Scripture.

Perhaps these "departers from the faith" are individuals who have been affected by the spirit of the age or the politically correct thinking of the day. Maybe they are individuals who have become weary because they've been hassled by a hostile and changing culture around them.

Regardless of the reason why, the Holy Spirit tells us that some in the Church will depart from the faith at the conclusion of the period — along with the rest of society that will be morally wandering.

These shocking prophetic utterances of Jesus and Paul were not intended to scare us; they were recorded to prepare and awaken us so that we'll stand strong. This has never been more true than for those living at the end of the age as this temptation to depart from truth tries to force its way throughout all of society, including the Church.

Since we are living at the tipping point of the age when this is prophesied to occur, you and I must predetermine that even if times drastically change and all of society turns in the wrong direction, the absolute veracity of Scripture is timeless and unchanging and will remain our guide. We must plant our feet firmly on the solid rock of God's Word and refuse to be moved by the spirit of seduction that is luring the rest of the world into many forms of deception.

HAS THE TIME THAT
WAS TO COME ALREADY ARRIVED?

In Second Timothy 4:3 and 4, Paul commented further about this last-days deception that would attempt to influence and affect the Church. He said, "For the time will come when they will not endure sound doctrine; but after their own lusts shall they heap to themselves teachers, having itching ears; and they shall turn away their ears from the truth, and shall be turned unto fables."

Even now, what Paul wrote about in these verses is already taking place as people gravitate toward teaching and preaching that is more psychological and philosophical than Bible-based. It is shocking to see how the Bible is slowly vanishing even in churches that were once considered to be solid Bible-teaching churches. Unless a turn in this trend occurs, what Paul prophesied in Second Timothy 4:3 and 4 will transpire right before our eyes. It appears to already be happening.

In some churches today, there is very little Bible teaching to awaken people's hearts and clear their obscured thinking. As a result, people are becoming biblically illiterate and spiritually numb — completely uninformed of what the Bible says concerning very serious issues. This is certainly not true of all churches, but it is a disturbing and growing trend.

I have great respect for those in Christian leadership who *are* staying with the Scriptures regardless of a changing moral climate. My appreciation for them — for their courage and commitment — is simply enormous. Concerning these precious men and women, I echo the deep sentiment of David: "The godly people in the land are my true heroes!..." (Psalm 16:3 *NLT*).

Paul continued to tell us in Second Timothy 4:3 and 4 that there would be an erring last-days group that would discard fixed truth and replace it with "fables" — the Greek word for *fantasies*.

By using the word "fables," Paul inferred that these last-days orators would substitute authentic teaching of the Bible for an emphasis that is not biblical. The demand for these fanciful messages will produce *newly fashioned* teachers with *restyled* messages.

In Matthew 24:5, Christ revealed that deception would be a *primary sign* that we've reached the final season of the age. According to Jesus, this deception will affect every part of society and it will spread across the globe like a growing cancer. Then in both First Timothy 4:1 and Second Timothy 4:3 and 4, Paul alerted us that even the Church would be affected by this spirit of deception and delusion — warning us that we must stick with the clear teaching of Scripture and strengthen ourselves in the Word of God.

Paul tells us in Second Timothy 4:2 that ministry in the pulpit is a holy and sacred position that we are to use to *"preach the Word."* But according to the Holy Spirit's prophetic declarations through the apostle in verses 3 and 4, many in pulpit ministry will gradually and subtly depart from the clear teaching of Scripture. They will gravitate more and more toward teaching and preaching that suits the ears of an erring generation.

YOU HAVE THE HOLY SPIRIT'S POWER TO REMAIN FAITHFUL!

The changes taking place in the world in the closing days will result in one of two choices for every believer: a decision to accommodate the world — or a refusal to compromise. *Riding the fence will no longer be an option.* Those who make no room for compromise may face the backlash of a society that grows increasingly intolerant of those who stand for moral absolutes. However, faithful and unwavering believers can also expect the empowering of the Holy Spirit to uphold them and cause them to ultimately triumph in Christ who gives them strength.

Never forget that you have the power of the Holy Spirit within you. If you'll surrender to His indwelling presence, He will give you the strength needed to remain faithful and unwavering in spite of a world that is changing all around you.

The moral climate is dramatically shifting, as Scripture prophesied it would at the conclusion of the age. But we who refuse to make room for compromise in our faith must hold our position with confidence, understanding that we have been ordained by God to live in this hour. We were chosen for this moment to demonstrate victorious living in Jesus Christ — *by His all-sufficient grace* — in a world that has run amuck.

We were chosen for this moment to demonstrate victorious living in Jesus Christ — *by His all-sufficient grace* — in a world that has run amuck.

What can you do to reinforce your faith and the faith of your family to withstand the forces of deception that are attempting to affect every part of society in these last days? Christ did not warn of this end-times sign to scare us — His intention was to *jar and jolt* us into spiritual sobriety so that we could protect ourselves against the spirit of deception that *will* be at work at the end of the age.

Think About It

1. Jesus' words "take heed" regarding a last-days deception were intended to *jar* and *jolt* the hearer. How does the Savior's warning against massive deception prompt *you* to mount a guard in your heart to avoid this spiritually toxic phenomenon?

2. Do you see instances in the news today, or in your surroundings, of society calling "evil good and good evil" (*see* Isaiah 5:20)? What are some of those instances?

3. Jesus said deception would be widespread in the world at the end of the age. How can a believer recognize the marks of deception in order to steer clear of it and remain useable in the hands of God?

Chapter Four

Wars, Rumors of Wars, and Commotions

Since the turn of the twentieth century, approximately 150 million lives have been lost across the globe as casualties of war.[1] That horrific statistic includes world wars, regional conflicts, and continual skirmishes in parts of the world renowned for political unrest. We've experienced wars, the threat of wars, and violent disturbances in our cities. Our society has been disrupted by rival governments, fringe militia, factions, and groups and individuals whose hatred drives them to commit unimaginable crimes.

These disturbances are no longer lurking in the distance. They have made their way to our own backyard, it seems. Reminiscent of the "duck and cover" air-raid drills conducted in classrooms in the 1950s, now people are receiving instructions on what to do if they find themselves in the vicinity of an active shooter.

Although some statistics cite that casualties of war and crime are currently in a mode of decline, Jesus nevertheless warned of all kinds of violent disturbances as a sign of the close of the age. In Matthew 24:6, He said, "...Ye shall hear of wars and rumors of wars...."

Although many wars have been fought throughout human history, Jesus prophesied that hostile conflicts would especially occur at the conclusion of the last days. He alerted His disciples *and us* to the fact that conflicts of all types would appear as a signal that we have entered the last season of the age.

ARMED CONFLICT 'THEN AND NOW'

War was nothing new to the world of the First Century. At the time Jesus spoke these words to His disciples, the lands that surrounded the Mediterranean Sea — and vast parts of Europe, the Middle East, and Northern Africa — had been conquered by the Roman army. Thousands of waves of Roman legions had rolled across the then-known world with their advanced war machinery and the finest combat weapons ever created up to that time. They swooped upon land after land, seizing them as new territories for the ever-expanding Roman Empire. They attacked nations — knocking them off their feet and destabilizing them — until those countries collapsed under fierce military pressure and were added to the list of territories subjugated by Roman authority.

Before these Roman conquests, there had been a host of other military takeovers conducted by Babylonians, Persians, Egyptians, Greeks, and others. The history of wars — and even the notion of multiple conflicts being fought simultaneously — was not a new concept to the disciples. So when Jesus spoke of war to them, He was not speaking in unfamiliar terms. His followers were very familiar with wars, especially those that had been fought during their lifetime.

The word "wars" in Matthew 24:6 is the plural form of a Greek word that describes *armed conflict* — which would include *battles*, *fights*, *skirmishes*, and *large-scale conflicts*. Jesus prophesied that before the climax of the age, small and large conflicts of all types would all occur simultaneously across the planet on a dimension such as never before experienced or known.

WARS, RUMORS OF WARS, AND *COMMOTIONS*

In Luke 21:9, where we find Jesus' same discourse to the disciples about end-time events, He also prophesied that there would be a rise in "commotions." That verse says, "But when ye shall hear of wars and *commotions*, be not terrified...."

The word "commotions" describes *instability as a result of upheavals of a societal, political, or militaristic nature*. It could include any activity that sends society reeling as a result of its unpredictable nature. Jesus said that when you hear of these things, "...Be not terrified...." This word "terrified" is a translation of a Greek word that means *to experience extreme horror or fright as the result of something that startles or alarms*.

In looking at Jesus' words about last-days events in Matthew and Mark, we find that Jesus essentially says the same thing (Matthew 24:6; Mark 13:7). And in Matthew, Mark, and Luke, the word "terrified" each time is a Greek word that means *to cry out in terror*. All of these verses could actually be rendered, *"Be not terrorized!"* This prohibition implies that being terrorized would be a real temptation for an end-times generation.

Just as war was rampant in the First Century, terrorist activity was also very widespread in the First Century because of localized rebellions against Roman authority. Organized terrorist uprisings occurred frequently in places where people had been subjugated by Roman powers. Those terrorist attacks were viewed as "war against the state." These surprise attacks were hard to predict, difficult to control — and they produced upheaval, fear, and terror that startled and alarmed the people.

In recent decades, the world has seen a variety of similar uprisings sweep across entire geographical areas. In each place where these revolutions have occurred, it has resulted in disturbances, upheavals, political instability, and the spawning of more insurgencies and revolts.

AN UPSURGE IN TERRORISM

It's difficult to keep an accurate count of how many revolutions have occurred in recent years. There seems to be an unleashing of demonic forces into the earth with a fury that refuses to be pacified. If there has ever been a time when it felt like all restraints have been thrown off, it is now. To one observing the news, it appears as if the lid has been taken off *Pandora's box* — and we seem to be coexisting in a warring, terroristic environment that is unprecedented in scope.

News media around the world regularly report incidents of terrorist activities. Reports from international intelligence agencies state that terrorism is escalating in an increasing number of nations.[2] The Middle East as well as much of Europe and America lie marred in the global path of these bloody attacks. Middle-Easterners, Europeans, Asians, Americans, Africans, and Australians — people from nearly every part of the planet — have all felt the murderous effects of war and terrorism.

The rise in this type of terrorist activity — "commotions" that strike alarm in people's hearts — is unprecedented in our lifetime. But long ago when Jesus told His disciples about signs they would see to indicate the conclusion of the age, He exactly described the warring and terroristic activities that have become so commonplace in recent times.

A detailed Internet search can show a documented history of terrorist acts over the past century in various countries of the world, many of which have been motivated by race, religion, politics, or even personal revenge. Few anticipated what has transpired on the planet in such a relatively short period.

The possibility of random terror attacks has come so close to our everyday lives that in many places — schools, grocery stores, malls, theaters, sports stadiums, and even churches — people are required to enter through metal detectors to ensure their well-being against someone with an intent to kill.

When Jesus described key signs that would be evidence of the very end of the age, He prophesied that these very kinds of "wars, rumors of wars, and commotions" would be another key to gauge where we are in time and to show that the age is drawing to a close.

> Few anticipated what has transpired on the planet in such a relatively short period. The possibility of random terror attacks has come so close to our everyday lives.

FEAR AND TERROR ARE NOT THE WILL OF GOD FOR YOU!

Many nations have experienced the brutality of terrorism and the suffering it brings. Most have become aware that no one is completely immune from this worldwide menace — and many sense the need to be vigilant about where they are traveling and what is happening around them while en route. Paying attention to your surroundings has never been more important. This is why it is vital for us to abide intentionally "under His wings" as we navigate a dangerous world around us (*see* Psalm 91:4).

These end-time happenings have the potential to alarm us. But as we saw in Matthew 24:6 and Mark 13:7, Jesus said, "Be not terrorized" by these events. Furthermore, the Holy Spirit told us through the apostle Paul, "...God hath not given us the spirit of fear; but of power, and of love, and of a sound mind" (2 Timothy 1:7). This unquestionably means fear and terror are *not* the will of God for His people — and that includes *you!*

With diligence and fervor, we are eagerly awaiting a move of the Holy Spirit and the reaping of a great harvest of souls before Christ returns.

As faith-filled believers, we can thankfully have a different perspective of the signs we're seeing that indicate Jesus will return soon. We know that we are living at the very end of the last days — in the last "minutes and seconds" of the age. With diligence and fervor, we are eagerly awaiting a move of the Holy Spirit and the reaping of a great harvest of souls before Christ returns (*see* James 5:7).

For believers who are knowledgeable of what the Lord prophesied, these startling and alarming events point to the overarching truth that our redemption indeed "draweth nigh" (*see* Luke 21:28).

THE SOUND OF WAR RINGING IN OUR EARS

But in addition to Jesus foretelling that "wars" and "commotions" would be characteristic of the end of the age (*see* Matthew 24:6, Mark 13:7, and Luke 21:9), Jesus said we would also hear of "rumors of wars."

The word "rumors" in Matthew 24:6 is from the Greek word used to describe an *ear*. By using this word, Jesus lets us know that a last-days generation will live with an *earful* of news and information about these events occurring around the world.

Jesus never said that we would personally *see* all these wars, revolts, and disturbances — but that we would *hear* about them.

The words of Jesus imply that an excess of information will be available for people to hear about these events as they happen across the globe. The original Greek text could actually be translated, "You will *continually* hear of wars." It presents the idea of a *nonstop flow* of information.

These wars and acts of terrorism may not necessarily occur in our own neighborhoods, states, or countries — but the *nonstop news* of these events will bring them right into our homes via television, Internet, radio, or other means of communication.

In generations raised with television and the Internet, the availability of information is more prolific than in any other time in history. This pervasive availability will cause ears to *ring* with the sounds of casualties and conflicts. Jesus declared that an *earful* of various types of conflicts will be one of the foremost signs that the finality of the age is approaching.

> Jesus declared that an *earful* of various types of conflicts will be one of the foremost signs that the finality of the age is approaching.

Since we are living in the closing days of this age, we are a generation who will have an earful of these events. Therefore, it is imperative that we grab hold of the peace of God and not allow apprehension, fear, or worry to control our minds.

NO ACCESS — *ENTRANCE DENIED!*

In Philippians 4:7, Paul wrote, "And the peace of God, which passeth all understanding, shall keep your hearts and minds through Christ Jesus." Especially in light of the things we may see or experience as part of a last-days generation, I feel the need to encourage you from this verse of Scripture. This verse *promises* that the peace of God will keep our hearts and minds *if we will yield to it*!

The word "keep" is a Greek word that was specifically used to portray soldiers who stood at the gates of a city to determine who was allowed inside and who was forbidden access. Usually armed soldiers stood at the main gate of a city — and it was their job to determine if someone would be admitted to the city or turned away. If the soldiers deemed a person dangerous or a menace to that city, they blocked his entrance and turned him away.

This is precisely the word the apostle Paul used in Philippians 4:7 to describe how the peace of God can keep our hearts and minds. God's peace — if we'll yield to it — will stand at the door of our hearts and minds to block the entrance of fear, panic, and alarm if any of these toxic intruders tries to enter in. God's peace — if it is permitted to do its job — will prohibit fearful thoughts from entering our minds, upsetting our emotions, and causing us to turn aside from our steadied position of faith, peace, and rest.

> God's peace — if it is permitted to do its job — will prohibit fearful thoughts from entering our minds, upsetting our emotions, and causing us to turn aside from our steadied position of faith, peace, and rest.

This means that the peace of God is a guard at the "gate" of *your* heart. When you're tempted to fear because of something you've seen or heard or because of nonstop information you've seen on television or read about on the Internet, don't give way to those tormenting thoughts. Instead, let the peace of God guard your heart and mind by blocking the entrance of menacing thoughts.

Especially in the last days when many tragic events are occurring around the world, we can be disturbed by what we see and by the news that constantly rings in our ears. While it's healthy to be informed about what is happening, we can never let the information received through our senses determine whether or not we'll remain in a state of peace. We must allow the peace of God to do its job of guarding the entrance to our hearts and minds against all illegal entry.

In Philippians 4:8, Paul wrote, "Finally, brethren, whatsoever things are true, whatsoever things are honest, whatsoever things are just, whatsoever things are pure, whatsoever things are lovely, whatsoever things are of good report; if there be any virtue, and if there be any praise, think on these things."

"Think on *these* things." Through these verses, God is saying that we're not to worry or be anxious about anything. Nor are we to focus our attention on — in thought, word, or deed — the chaos in the world around us. Instead, we must focus on the truths and the promises in His Word.

Jesus is our Peace — and He will keep us in perfect peace when we trust Him and fix our minds on Him (*see* Ephesians 2:14; Isaiah 26:3). We must not be gripped with panic or alarm concerning the catastrophic events we're constantly hearing about in the news.

Remember that Jesus' purpose for telling us about all these signs in advance was not to *scare* us. His intention was to *prepare* us for victorious living in these last times. When panic or fear tries to assault us, we have to let peace stand in front of our hearts and minds as a guard — and our mouths must declare in agreement: *"ACCESS DENIED!"*

Jesus did not appoint us to live at the very end of the last days so we would fret and worry as we await His return. That's why Jesus said prohibitively: *"Be not troubled."* Jesus left us no option if we want to obey Him — He *commanded* us not to be afraid! Jesus emphatically meant, *"Do not be troubled, disturbed, panicked, or inwardly alarmed."*

THE END IS NOT YET

After He said, "...See that ye be not troubled...," Jesus continued, "...For all these things must come to pass, *but the end is not yet"* (Matthew 24:6).

Although "wars, rumors of wars, and commotions" are clear signs that we are living in the end of this age, there are *more* events to come before the completion of the age takes place. That is why Jesus said, "...The end is not by and by" (Luke 21:9). The word "end" means *immediate* or *imminent.* Although these events seem horrific, they are not the *final* signals that the age will be ending imminently. Jesus said there will be other signs to see as we near the ultimate conclusion of the era.

There will also be a great outpouring of the Holy Spirit in the last part of the last days — a move of the Spirit like never seen before. Those who maintain hungry hearts for the things of God — who are ready to be His hands and feet *and His voice* to a last-days generation — will participate in this great move of the Spirit. This is God's promise (*see* Acts 2:17,18), and it should ignite our faith to expect it to come to pass!

But for now, let's move on to the next chapter, where we will see that Jesus prophesied nations rising against nations, and kingdoms against kingdoms — *additional* precursors to the summation of the age.

Think About It

1. In what ways does the "sound of war" ring in our ears today compared to the way news of battles and conflicts was received in years past? Does this constant news of war incite alarm in your emotions or stir faith in your heart — or perhaps *both* at times? Or does this constant influx of news have a numbing effect on your mind concerning the violence and atrocities that are occurring in "some other" part of the world?

2. God has not given us the spirit of fear (*see* 2 Timothy 1:7). What steps can you take to process news of war through the filter of God's Word and to *keep* yourself in a constant state of His deep, abiding peace?

Chapter Five

Nation Against Nation, Kingdom Against Kingdom

In Matthew 24:7, Jesus continued explaining the signs that would be obvious as we traveled forward on a prophetic road toward the end of the age. He said that as we near the end of this period of time, "...Nation shall rise against nation, and kingdom shall rise against kingdom...."

As generations reflect on the past, true history will have recorded our own time as a moment when mayhem rocked many parts of the planet, perhaps on a wider scale than ever before. From natural appearances, it looks like an array of nations, races, religions, political parties, and ideologies is locked into a collision course against one another. As never before, it seems that nations are rising against nations and kingdoms against kingdoms! In this chapter, I will explain in further detail both of these phrases — "nation against nation" and "kingdom against kingdom" — and I believe you will see very clearly what I mean.

Despite all the uprisings today of one faction against another, it is worth noting what historians have pointed out about the time of the New Testament when Jesus prophesied about the clashing of nations and kingdoms. In reality, nations were *already* rising up against other nations, and kingdoms were *already* in conflict with one another. Jesus knew that, of course, yet He said, "…Nation *shall* rise against nation, and kingdom *shall* rise against kingdom…."

The word "shall" is used twice in this verse and prophetically points to events that *will occur in the future* — not to events that were already happening in Jesus' time, or in that day and hour. Jesus was predicting that "nation *shall* rise against nation, and kingdom *shall* rise against kingdom" (*see* Matthew 24:7; Mark 13:8; Luke 21:10).

This "rising against" describes *upheavals, confusion, disorder, turmoil,* and *instability* that will be stirred across the world at the very end of the age. It depicts a *seething* among the nations as a clear and authenticating sign that we are nearing the end of an era and that Jesus' return is near.

Jewish rabbis of Jesus' day taught that in the time just before the coming of the Messiah, conflicts and wars would be stirred up in the world. These rabbis declared that when we saw kingdom rising against kingdom, and one realm against another realm, it would be a signal to expect the imminent arrival of the Messiah.

Of course, the Jewish people of Jesus' day were awaiting the *first* coming of the Messiah. Many did not recognize Jesus as the One they were waiting for, nor that the "the day of their visitation" had already arrived (*see* Luke 13:34). Nonetheless, these rabbinic teachers correctly predicted that *chaos* would emerge and increase among the nations as a precursor to the end of an age and the coming of the Lord!

NATION AGAINST NATION, KINGDOM AGAINST KINGDOM

RACIAL AND ETHNIC CONFLICT
IN THE WORLD

There is something very important in the Greek that adds even more meaning to this end-time scenario in Matthew 24:7. The word "nation" in Greek is where we get the word *ethnic*. This means Jesus was actually forecasting a time when *ethnic groups* would rise up against other *ethnic groups*.

Has there ever been a time when there was more ethnic conflict than we've seen in contemporary history? In the more recent past, such conflicts were notably localized — but today, ethnic conflict is spreading like a disease across the planet. Increasing ethnic tensions and turmoil can be found on the streets of America, Europe, Africa, the Middle East, and in every part of the world.

One might think such conflicts, especially involving race, would decrease as time moves forward. Multitudes of people have suffered bigotry, injustice, and hardships for many years to see laws changed to bring equal rights to all races. Yet racial conflicts still seem to be *escalating*. In fact, tensions have risen on many fronts to a boiling point.

CONFLICT OVER RELIGION AND POLITICS

There is another type of upheaval that from almost the beginning has been prevalent all over the world. I'm talking about the conflicts that exist between *religions*.

One example of this that is becoming more and more predominant is the conflict between Shiite Muslims and Sunni Muslims. Although they both claim Islam as their faith, these groups are fiercely opposed to each other, and they engage in murderous warfare against one another. The bloodbath between these two groups is horrific. Could this also be an example of the end-time ethnic conflicts Jesus was predicting when He said that ethnic groups would rise against ethnic groups at the very end of days?

Those who work in international affairs are well aware that these conflicts are getting worse — whether it's racial tensions in the United States, conflicting tribes in Africa, Muslim factions in the Middle East, antagonism between nations in Europe, or ethnic issues in other parts of the world. Furthermore, these conflicts are more difficult to resolve than in years past. It seems to all be leading to a less controlled, less predictable world. As power becomes more diffused and antagonism among regional powers intensifies — rendering resolutions to these conflicts becomes even more complex.[1]

If a list of ethnic conflicts that are occurring right now were compiled, it could fill several pages. This is simply a time when conflicts among ethnic groups have erupted across vast regions of the earth. This eruption is spilling over into other regions like a plague, and it is causing national and international threats to previously peaceful parts of the world.

Jesus prophesied the stirring of *ethnic groups* — including racial, religious, and political groups and factions — in the very last days.

Jesus prophesied the stirring of *ethnic groups* — including racial, religious, and political groups and factions — in the very last days. Regardless of the cause, it is clear that these contentions are happening with greater frequency in our day. The fact that these uprisings are occurring on a greater scale confirms Jesus' words and sounds a clear signal that we are approaching the very end of the age.

VIOLENT FORCE AND A LUST FOR SUPERIORITY

Jesus said, "...Nation shall rise *against* nation..." (Matthew 24:7). The word "against" is the Greek word *epi*. It adds the idea of *force*. Jesus was forecasting a time when nations or ethnic groups would *forcibly* or *violently* rise up against other groups.

The word *epi* also means *upon*, and in this sense, it depicts one group trying to gain *superiority* over another. We've seen this in the Middle East, but it is also raging and on the rise among various religions and races across the world.

Human wisdom will never prevail over the seething contentions that challenge the world today. Only the wisdom and power of God manifested through His people will push back the dark forces that instigate these conflicts — and rescue many who are perishing amidst the bloody turmoil.

It's also important to point out that many such commotions and conflicts contribute to people being displaced and plagued with hunger and famine, which we will look at in the following chapter. The fallout that occurs in the aftermath of conflict, including the rise of refugees living in destitution, is not something that happened only long ago. It's happening right now across the globe — and Jesus foretold it as a sign that would alert us to His imminent return.

Jesus' prophetic words in Matthew 24:7 plainly tell us that nations will rise against nations, ethnic conflicts will escalate, and they will gather speed and proliferate across the planet as we race toward the close of the age. This is one of the signs Jesus gave so that believers would know that the very end is indeed near.

UNCIVIL POLITICS

But after Jesus told His disciples, "...Nation shall rise against nation...," He added, "...And kingdom shall rise against kingdom..." (Matthew 24:7).

Again, we see the word "against" used in this phrase — from the Greek word *epi* — indicating *force* or a desire to take a *superior, dominant* position over another. The word "kingdom" in Matthew 24:7 refers to *a dominion or realm of power and influence*. The word "kingdoms" could present the idea of *nations, political parties, alliances*, and even *ideological factions* maneuvering for superiority over the other at the very end of this age.

Jesus foretold that "kingdom *shall* rise against kingdom" toward the end of the age. Again, the word *shall* is used in this verse to prophetically point to events that *will occur in the future* — not to events that were already happening in Jesus' time. Jesus was speaking of something that would occur in a significant way in the future, toward the conclusion of the age.

To understand what Jesus was talking about, we could reflect on the political behavior we are seeing today. We may be witnessing the most uncivil politics in contemporary history. We are watching one party or affiliation not only try to gain superiority over another — but they also seem to be trying to decimate one another in the process! It is the clashing of one realm against another realm — one ideology against another ideology — as each tries to doom the other. This scramble for superiority at almost any cost alerts us that our culture has taken a nosedive in terms of civility.

None of this is news to those of us who have been watching ugly politics on our TV screens, computers, or mobile devices. Has there ever been a time in our age when political parties and various warring ideologies have been more uncivil? The public behavior of politicians and political parties has departed from the days of respectful disagreement into an ugly mess of intolerance and mudslinging. Add to that a widespread weaponizing of the media to perpetuate this indecent assault, and you have a modern picture of "kingdom rising again kingdom."

Jesus prophesied in no uncertain terms what would occur before the end of the age and His return. Now let's turn to the next sign He gave us: *famines and economic instability.* As you will see, it is an end-time prediction of scarcity of all types in the last days.

Think About It

1. Contemplate examples of modern-day "nations rising against nations" — including the acts of certain racial, religious, and political groups and factions. What is the role of believers amidst incidents of racism, religious wars, and political mudslinging and undermining of others?

2. How can you more readily permit God's power, wisdom, goodness, and love to flow through you to push back dark spiritual forces that are instigating conflict throughout the world? How should the Church prepare in this day to reap the last of the "precious fruit of the earth" — *souls* — for whom Christ died?

Chapter Six

Famine, Hunger, Scarcity, and Economic Woes

When the disciples asked Jesus for the sign of His coming, Jesus also foretold that *shortages, scarcities, hunger,* and *deficits* of all types would upset the world at the very end of the age just before He returned.

Jesus had already warned about massive deception, wars, terrorism (commotions), nations rising against nations, and kingdoms clashing with other kingdoms. But He continued His discourse on end-time events by telling His disciples, "…And there shall be *famines*…" (Matthew 24:7).

Famines are certainly not new, as there have been many notable famines in world history. But according to Jesus' words in Matthew 24:7, there will be a scarcity of food in many parts of the world toward the end of this era just before He returns.

In the next pages, we'll look a little deeper at the Greek text in Matthew 24:7 to see what is included in this word "famine." After all, this is a word Christ Himself used to describe events that will occur as the age wraps up and comes to a close.

The word "famines" in Matthew 24:7 comes from a Greek word that literally describes *scarcity of grain*. Because the word used in this verse is *plural,* it depicts *multiple famines* and *multiple scarcities* that will occur simultaneously in various parts of the earth at the very end of the age. Because "famine" describes a scarcity of grain, it is assumed by most readers that this refers only to *physical* hunger — and it is absolutely true that Jesus was prophesying that a time of *great physical hunger* would develop in nations of the world toward the very end of the period. But as you will see, the Greek word for "famine" includes much more than that.

First, however, let's look at the facts regarding world hunger in our time.

WORLD HUNGER TODAY — THE ALARMING FACTS

The following information is written to give you a brief overview of the recent conditions of hunger in the world today. Because this overview is based on statistics that are valid at the time I am writing this book, it may fall short of the real picture by the time this book comes into your hands. The numbers concerning world hunger are unfortunately growing *exponentially.*

According to a report from *2016 World Hunger and Poverty Facts and Statistics,* more than 250,000 people die every year around the world from hunger and hunger-related causes.[1] Another shocking report is that between 250,000 to 500,000 children become blind each year due to vitamin deficiency caused by extreme undernourishment — and half of those die within a year of their blindness.[2] Besides the people who actually starve to death, millions more languish in undernourished conditions. Instead of living with vibrancy and hope for the future, their lives have halted to a standstill as they focus solely on where to obtain food for themselves and their loved ones so they can continue to subsist.

Think of the famines that have purged millions of people from the planet in various parts of the world — even in our lifetime. The images of starving children and adults have been paraded before us on television and other media to bring the stark reality of this suffering to the forefront of our minds. In many parts of the world, the lack of food and clean water — or the lack of any water at all — is an unimaginable crisis. Despite the wonderful efforts by many charitable organizations, the problems associated with hunger, malnutrition, and disease as a result of no water or dirty water has grown worse in recent years.[3]

Currently our planet has a population of approximately 7.6 billion people. According to the Food and Agriculture Organization of the United Nations, approximately 1 in 9 — or about 815,000,000 people — suffer from chronic undernourishment.[4] That means all these people lack the food necessary to maintain normal health. To help you understand the approximate size of that number, think of the population *of the entire European continent* — and then add to that the populations of California and Texas *combined*!

Let's more closely define what the word "undernourishment" means. The following four points explain the various nuances of this word:

1. To be nourished with less than the minimum amount of food essential for normal health and growth.

2. To be deprived of the essential elements required for one's normal and healthy development.

3. To live on an insufficient quantity or quality of nourishment that is needed to maintain ongoing health and growth.

4. To have insufficient amounts of food to remain in good health.

As I have stated, currently 815,000,000 people are living on less than the minimum amount of food essential for health, growth, and life. In other words, these 815,000,000 people are *starving*. The greatest number affected are children.

Worse still, according to studies within the last five years, globally 51 million children under the age of five are "wasted," meaning they have an abnormally low weight-to-height ratio.[5] Of that number, 17 million — *that's fully one third* — are *severely* wasted, meaning the condition is fatal.[6] The term "wasted" depicts a person so undernourished that he is dangerously thin, and sickness is caused as a result. Of course, eventually these children will experience *death* if food and medical care are not provided.

> Currently 815,000,000 people are living on less than the minimum amount of food essential for health, growth, and life. The greatest number affected are children.

Making matters even worse, hunger creates a vicious cycle. Malnutrition produces poor health, which results in abnormally small body sizes, low levels of energy, and a marked reduction in mental functions. These factors lead only to more poverty. Those suffering are so affected physically that they are not able to learn or to work as adults because their bodies are deprived of needed nutrients and vitamins. All of this downward progression promotes a seemingly unending cycle of even greater hunger.

The facts about poverty are alarming and disheartening. A study of this information makes it very clear why God hates poverty. These statistics expose poverty's true nature as a thief that steals time, focus, energy, talent, and even life itself. Simply stated, poverty leads to hunger — *and hunger leads to more poverty*. Without intervention to stop this sequence of events, the cycle will be unending. What poverty produces is simply devastating — a truth that cannot be exaggerated.

WARS AND CONFLICTS — CONTRIBUTORS TO THE HUNGER PROBLEM

In Chapter Five, we saw what Jesus prophesied about wars, rumors of wars, commotions, and conflicts — and we saw how they have been emerging on a massive scale, just as He said they would in the last days. But now let's see how all of these military conflicts contribute to advance the horrible condition of world hunger.

A world at war produces one worldwide calamity after another, one of which is famine and shortages of food. Many factors contribute to food shortfalls in different parts of the world, but the impact of wars and ethnic, political, and religious conflicts is huge on this heartbreaking issue of famine and hunger.

Exacerbating the hunger issue is the growing number of displaced people who live in countries rife with continued conflicts and fighting. As political and religious ideologies collide on an increasing level, the number of refugees is increasing commensurately, and the problem of impoverishment and hunger is growing right along with it.

Right now there are more than one billion people on the earth who earn less than $1.25 a day.[7] These meager earnings make it almost impossible for them to purchase even small "doses" of food to sustain their lives. World hunger is being felt all over the planet — and it is a sign that Jesus said we would witness just before the end of the age.

WHAT CAN WE DO TO HELP COMBAT THIS END-TIMES PROBLEM?

As Christians, most of us understand at varying levels that it is our job to combat the forces of darkness in this world — through prayer, our walk of humility and obedience before God, the proclamation of His Word, etc. But we must also make the effort to combat these dark forces through more natural means. I'm talking about something as simple as opening our wallets and sharing our resources with those in need!

Just reading the information in these paragraphs should be enough to compel us to seek ways to help those who are in need if we are not already doing so. The Bible is full of scriptures about helping the poor and hungry — and promises special blessings to those who obey God's charge to make a difference in the lives of people in need.

> The Bible is full of scriptures about helping the poor and hungry — and promises special blessings to those who obey God's charge to make a difference in the lives of people in need.

Even if we feel that *we* are struggling financially, compared to many other parts of the earth, we are blessed! And those who are blessed more than others have a God-given responsibility to hear the cry of the poor (*see* Proverbs 21:13). We are obligated to do something to make a difference in the lives of suffering people.

If sacrificing financially on behalf of the hungry and needy seems like a daunting goal for you, I'm wondering — would you consider denying yourself a meal once a week and sending the equivalent of that expenditure to a Gospel ministry that feeds the poor? *In some places, the cost of one hamburger, a side of fries, and a soft drink could feed an undernourished person for a whole week!*

I encourage you to consider making this kind of small investment into the lives of those who lack the basic provision of adequate food to sustain health and growth. This type of compassionate, sacrificial act will bring a special blessing from God to your life. Proverbs 19:17 declares, "He that hath pity upon the poor, lendeth unto the Lord; and that which he hath given will he pay him again."

Living in the last days provides opportunities for each of us to reach out and make a difference in the lives of those who are suffering the effects of famine and hunger. Most of these hungry people never asked to be put into these situations. Nevertheless, they live in dire circumstances that are beyond their control. They barely subsist in chaos-affected homes or conflict-affected regions, where fighting, instability, and upheavals of all kinds have caused them to be deprived of basic sustenance for daily living.

Whether our offering is big or small, we must each recognize our responsibility to contribute in some way to make a difference in the lives of people who are undernourished, impoverished, or starving.

ECONOMIC WOES — THE END-TIME SHAKING CONTINUES

The horrendous facts of global hunger demand our prayers and our actions, but there is more we must see about this word "famines" as it was used in early New Testament times. What else did this word mean in Jesus' time — and what does it mean for the days in which we live?

As noted at the beginning of this chapter, the word "famine" specifically described *a scarcity of grain*. The economies of Jesus' day were largely based on grain. That is one reason why nations like Egypt were considered such rich countries — Egypt, in particular, was a *huge* source of grain in the world at that time. Just think what would have happened if that country had experienced a "famine" of grain in Jesus' day. A scarcity like that could have plunged the economies of the civilized world into chaos.

In the ancient world, to a large extent, economies were based on grain, so a shortage of grain would have resulted in an economic *shaking*. It would have produced a worldwide crisis similar to the shaking we experience in our own day when the value of stocks plummets in a stock market. A shortage of grain would have financially debilitated the Roman Empire in much the same way a crash in the trade markets would affect the world today.

Since so much of the economic system of Jesus' time was based on grain, that system could very well be compared to the commodities that are sold and traded today as a basis for *our* world economy. Because of the financial impact this one resource had on the entire Roman Empire, one might say grain was like the "stock exchange" of the ancient world!

So when Jesus used "famines" to forecast a scarcity of grain and widespread hunger in the last days, He was additionally forecasting that a time would come at the end of the age when economic shortfalls and deficits would be so immense that these *famines* would affect global economies. This was a prediction of *financial instability* at the end of the age.

Mark's gospel adds an additional word to this prediction of end-time famines that will give us more insight into Christ's prediction of financial instability in the last days. In Mark 13:8, the writer recorded that Jesus said, "...There shall be famines and *troubles....*"

The word "troubles" is from a Greek word that means to be *troubled, stirred up, agitated, anxious,* or *upset*. It could be translated as the word "distress," thus picturing people who are *distressed* about something deeply disturbing or troubling.

Because Jesus used the word "famine" — or *scarcity* — in the plural form, He let us know that such financial shakings would be repeated *again and again*. He was prophetically forecasting that financial instability would become more and more common as we draw closer to the end of the age. In other words, the earth at that time in history would exist in a state of being *financially troubled, stirred up, agitated, anxious, and upset.*

So in addition to hunger itself, Jesus was also forecasting *deficits, economic shortages,* and *financial hardships* will affect the earth and serve as another indicator that we are speeding toward the close of the age and the soon return of Christ for His Church.

SHOULD *THIS* PREDICTION FRIGHTEN US?

Regardless of what has transpired in the world at any given season in history, God's people have always been preserved. It will be no different for believers in the last days who embrace their "better covenant, which was established upon better promises" (*see* Hebrews 8:6). Our faith and trust in Christ's words — and careful attention to His leading — will hold us steady through any storm of scarcity that affects society and global financial markets in this end-times age.

> Our faith and trust in Christ's words — and careful attention to His leading — will hold us steady through any storm of scarcity that affects society and global financial markets in this end-times age.

At the close of the age, people will experience what no other population in history has seen or experienced. Because of this, it is essential that we keep our eyes locked on the promises of God's Word for every sphere of our lives.

Now let's move to the next chapter, where we will see that Jesus prophesied about *pestilence* and *emerging diseases* at the end of the age just before He returns.

Think About It

1. What did you learn about the word Jesus used for "famines" in terms of its broader meaning beyond just "food shortages"? How might "famines" apply today in the economy where you live, and also worldwide, in this modern day?

2. If you haven't already done so, consider laying out a plan for contributing in some way toward situations of hunger and poverty, whether locally or globally. Perhaps it will mean not enjoying the purchase of a daily coffee or simply cutting back on eating out throughout the month in order to implement your plan. Ask the Lord to help you settle on a doable strategy and then be faithful to carry it out.

3. War can have an immediate, direct effect of devastation and displacement in people's lives. Contemplate how war and other types of conflict that disrupt a society can *indirectly* result in poverty, hunger, and, ultimately, death by starvation.

Chapter Seven

The Emergence of Pestilences and New Diseases

Jesus forewarned that at the very end of the age, there would be an emergence and proliferation of *diseases*. He said, "*There shall be pestilences*" (*see* Matthew 24:7).

The word "pestilence" is a Greek medical term that described *disease*. However, in Matthew 24:7, the word is used in its *plural* form. This means Jesus predicted that a phenomenon would develop at the end of the age in which *multiple* sicknesses and diseases would simultaneously appear.

Many different kinds of pestilences have emerged over the centuries, but in Matthew 24:7, as well as in Luke 21:11, Jesus prophesied about sicknesses and diseases, *plural*, to let us know that numerous such diseases would emerge in the very last days.

The planet is already being hard-hit with multiple diseases that are decimating populations all over the world. Even if cures exist, medicines and supplies to deal with the avalanche of disease spreading throughout the human race are often in short supply.

In addition to normal strains of disease that medical science regularly combats, today science is struggling to fight the onslaught of *newly emerging infectious diseases*. These are often actually old diseases that have had life breathed into them again. Such reemerging diseases have the potential to affect massive populations across the earth.[1] Cures for these are frequently more difficult to find as new strains of the diseases become more powerful, and as a result, larger numbers of people are put at risk.

In Matthew 24:7 and Luke 21:11 as Jesus was describing signs that we have entered the very last days of the age, He distinctly prophesied that at the end of the age, diseases — *plural* — would emerge and, thus, multitudes of lives could be affected.

Since we are living at the time of the last of the last days, it behooves us to know exactly what the Bible promises regarding healing. This is our moment as the Church to rise up with authority to pray for the sick with confidence, backed up by healing promises from the Bible. Jesus clearly prophesied that at the end of the age, the world would be battered by demonic powers that long to ravage, ruin, and *devastate* people's health and lives. Because we have the promises of the Word of God and the power of the Spirit, we are equipped to answer His call to bring healing to the sick at the end of this age.

ILL-PREPARED FOR THE MASS EFFECT

As advanced as the field of health sciences has become, it is not ready to deal with the massive effect of multiple newly emerging diseases. This state of being ill-prepared was observed in recent years when the Ebola virus hit western Africa and thousands died horrific, painful deaths.[2]

The U.N.'s *World Health Organization* (WHO) states that many potential epidemic and pandemic pestilences already exist in latent states. This means many life-threatening diseases are lying dormant and could be awakened at any moment to swiftly invade the human race. If even one or two of these epidemics became activated and found a way into the world's population, what could happen in a very brief period of time is unthinkable.[3] The mere thought of this possibility has scientists and the medical world in a constant state of urgency.

The *World Health Organization* defines an "emerging disease" as one that appears in a population for the first time — *or* one that may have existed previously, but is rapidly increasing in incidence or geographic range.[4] The website of WHO reports:

"In this stage of history, professionals predict that directly before us will be the emergence of new infectious diseases and that the reemergence of 'old' diseases will have a significant impact on health. A number of factors will influence this development: travel and trade, microbiological resistance, human behavior, breakdowns in health systems, and increased pressure on the environment. Social, political, and economic factors that cause the movement of people will increase contact between people and microbes, and environmental changes caused by human activity all will contribute to the spread of disease. The overuse of antibiotics and insecticides, combined with inadequate or deteriorating public health infrastructures, will hamper or delay responses to increasing disease threats."[5]

It is already a fact that infectious, communicable diseases are on the rise.[6] With the increase of sexual promiscuity, science projects that sexually transmitted infections (STIs) and diseases will spread like a forest fire burning out of control. This broad category of disease is already a raging inferno that is affecting the whole world. There are no known cures for some of these sexually transmitted infections. Through the use of prescription medications, some of them can be managed and outbreaks can be prevented or minimized. But even in a "managed" state, STIs remain contagious and continue to be spread from partner to partner — making this a pandemic development.

A pandemic, or pandemic disease, is an outbreak that potentially affects *world populations*. For example, if a new or reemerging viral strain erupted that could easily circulate among humans, such a virus could rage across the planet as a pandemic. Medical monitoring organizations around the world — such as the *Health Protection Agency* (HPA) in the UK, the *World Health Organization* (WHO), and the *Centers for Disease Control and Prevention* (CDC) — monitor the movements of such viruses. These organizations are responsible for standing alert and vigilant at the prospect of pandemics that could break out among the human populace.

A supreme example of a pandemic in history would be the Black Death, or "The Plague," one of the most devastating in human history. This plague resulted in the deaths of an estimated 50 million people, peaking in Europe in the years 1346-53.[7] In addition to this world-renowned case, mankind throughout history has experienced many other pandemics that cumulatively have annihilated millions.

THE PANDEMIC OF HIV AND AIDS

Although it is not discussed as much in the media as it was decades ago, HIV (Human Immunodeficiency Virus) is one of the most serious pandemics in the world. HIV causes death — 35,000,000 deaths from 1981 up to the time of this writing[8] — and serious health issues for a large number of the earth's population.

Worldwide there are approximately 2,000,000 new cases of HIV each year.[9] At the time this book is being published, approximately 36,700,000 people are living with HIV around the world.[10] But it won't be long until this statistic becomes obsolete as the disease continues to spread.

Most of us know that AIDS (Acquired Immune Deficiency Syndrome or Acquired Immunodeficiency Syndrome) is a condition caused by the virus known as HIV. AIDS develops as an opportunistic infection in a person infected with HIV. Both of these diseases were first identified by the scientific community in the early 1980s.[11] HIV affects the immune system, making sufferers much more vulnerable to infections and diseases. This susceptibility worsens as the disease progresses, and there is currently no medical cure for HIV or AIDS.

HIV is commonly known to be found in the body fluids of an infected person, such as in semen, blood, and breast milk — and is passed from person to person through blood-to-blood and sexual contact. Pregnant women can even pass HIV to their babies in the womb or during childbirth. Therefore we know that HIV can be transmitted in various ways, such as through vaginal, oral, or anal sex, blood transfusions, and contaminated hypodermic needles, etc.

I don't want to write in any more graphic detail than I already have. I simply wanted to share one example of a current pandemic that is growing faster than researchers can keep up with. Its ferocity has struck the human race with a vengeance — *with no present medical cure to stop it.*

Medical treatments for HIV are aggressive and costly with no guarantee of recovery. Although many are surviving HIV with expensive drugs and medical monitoring to mitigate this disease, the fact remains that if a diagnosis of AIDS follows, it is ultimately a *death sentence* without miraculous intervention. Medical breakthroughs have been invented that slow the process, but without more advancements in science — or without divine intervention — death is the scientifically irrefutable outcome of this diagnosis.

Sub-Saharan Africa bears the heaviest burden of HIV/AIDS worldwide.[12] In fact, this region of the world accounts for 69 percent of all new HIV infections recorded.[13] By the year 2014, half of all adolescents diagnosed with HIV *in the world* were living in just six countries — South Africa, Nigeria, Kenya, India, Mozambique, and Tanzania![14] All of those nations, with the exception of India, are located in this Sub-Saharan region. If you add this disheartening statistic to the extreme famine that also exists in that part of the world, you will see that Sub-Saharan Africa is under a horrible assault on many fronts.

Other regions significantly affected by HIV/AIDS include much of Asia (with India ranking third largest in the world for HIV infections[15]), the Pacific territories, Latin America, the Caribbean, and parts of Europe, including regions of the former Soviet Union. HIV and AIDS continue to spread and decimate populations around the globe.

As long as illicit behaviors continue on the planet — such as intravenous drug addiction, homosexuality, and sex outside of marriage — this problem will continue. But God has lovingly provided a remedy through Jesus Christ in His sacrificial act of redemption. And He gives people His unchanging Word to guide their lives, to empower them to live godly in Christ, and to heal them of every affliction and disease.

When Christ died on the Cross, nothing was left undone in God's amazing redemptive plan for humanity. His compassion

> God has lovingly provided a remedy through Jesus Christ in His sacrificial act of redemption. And He gives people His unchanging Word to guide their lives, to empower them to live godly in Christ, and to heal them of every affliction and disease.

is great toward all — *including* those ravaged by the effects of disobedient choices and sin.

INFECTED AND UNAWARE

HIV and AIDS have also taken its toll on the United States. More than 1.2 million people in America were living with HIV at the end of 2012, the most recent year at the time of this writing for which new and conclusive information is available to the public.[16] What is really horrifying is that, of those people who contracted HIV, *3 in 10 did not know they were infected!*[17]

Shockingly, a sexually active category of people infected with HIV — those who regularly have sex with multiple partners — is a younger generation of people approximately 13-24 years old. In 2016, young people in this age category accounted for more than 1 in 5 new HIV diagnoses.[18] As you will see, it's often those in this category who are also not informed that they're infected.

If you follow this line of thinking to its logical conclusion, you can see that as the sexual behavior of this group continues, infected people will unknowingly spread this deadly disease *from partner to partner to partner*. Each newly infected person will unknowingly spread it to the next sexual partner, and so on. It's not difficult to see that the scenario is serious beyond exaggeration.

An HIV-infected individual becomes contagious almost immediately upon contracting the virus, but the disease *can* potentially remain latent for approximately ten years before the person develops symptoms.[19] This latency period is actually "evolutionary" for the virus as it strengthens itself in that state so it can survive and reproduce.[20] You can see how this disease can spread *exponentially* — while it is yet latent or hidden — before even one person becomes aware he or she has been afflicted.

In light of these statistics, it is likely that you know someone who is infected with HIV and is unaware of it. According to the most recent reports, among people aged 13-24, an estimated 44 percent of those infected with HIV don't know they've contracted this incurable disease![21]

At a time when this disease is ravaging the world, a lost world system has placed its stamp of approval upon illicit behaviors in order to be "politically correct" in an inclusive society. Meanwhile, HIV/AIDS and STIs are growing and spreading in pandemic proportions — and the casualties of this war on human lives are astronomical.

WHO CONTRACTS HIV?

In the year 2014, the most recent year for reliable statistics concerning HIV/AIDS, gay and bisexual men accounted for 67 percent of all new HIV diagnoses in the United States. In the same year, individuals infected through heterosexual sex made up 24 percent of all new diagnoses. Additionally, about 13 percent of new cases occurred as a result of intravenous drug use among homosexual and heterosexual males and females, and by *in utero* transmission from mother to child.[22]

In the 13-24 year-old category, males who have sex with men are especially affected by HIV, as I've already mentioned. In 2014, young gay and bisexual men accounted for 92 percent of all new HIV diagnoses in this age category.[23]

Jesus clearly proclaimed that "pestilences" — whether they are sexually transmitted diseases or outbreaks of old and new diseases — would be an indicator we are nearing the wrap-up of the present age. He told us about this sign in advance to prepare us for what lies ahead in a last-days society. Jesus' desire is that we would renew our minds with His Word, avoid sins of the flesh, and learn how to receive His protection from these deadly catastrophes.

We have already seen that spiritual and moral deception will be a chief sign that we are living at the end of the age. As a result of the moral confusion that is already exerting its influence in society, many are misguided and afflicted. The manifestation of sicknesses and diseases as a result is more evidence of a society run amuck.

GOD'S TESTED DESIGN
FOR YOUR PROTECTION!

In order to write this chapter, I did a lot of research, with help from medical professionals, about which diseases really have the attention of the CDC and WHO. When I saw the list of emerging infectious diseases these organizations had compiled, I found the information to be nearly overwhelming.

Although the combined efforts of many organizations are attempting to bring this under control, there simply is no organization, nation, or group of medical professionals adequate to deal with the suffering that is rippling across the planet even now because of multiple newly emerging diseases. It is simply beyond human capacity to conquer the menacing viruses and plagues that are emerging and reemerging. And as bleak as the picture already is, it does not even include the diseases that are anticipated to arise in the future.

Those who walk by faith in the promises of God's Word are assured of divine protection and health as they renew their minds to these divine words of truth and learn to cooperate with God's spiritual laws of blessing and protection. But it is also essential that people, young and old alike, are taught abstinence before marriage and to maintain lives of sexual purity — not only for the sake of godliness, but also for the sake of a disease-free life for themselves and others.

Those who choose to participate in sexual promiscuity may think they're enjoying sin for a season (*see* Hebrews 11:25), but the truth is that they are playing a dangerous game with their lives. The immediate gratification of the flesh outside of God's prescribed laws for marriage is potentially lethal in these days at the end of the age.

The book of Proverbs is filled with God's wisdom for everyday life — from fidelity in marriage and wisdom in relationships to being excellent in our work and dealing honestly in business. If you're not already doing so, you might consider reading one chapter in this book of the Bible every day. It's a practice that will help undergird you with wisdom, strength, and protection in these times.

Another important step to ensure that you have victory over temptation is to maintain a network of godly support. Rather than try to "go it alone" in a world where morals have been thrown to the wind, why not join a support system of friends who can hold you accountable to your commitment to maintain a sexually pure life?

A network of godly friends can help you stay on track with the Lord and assist you as you move forward to fulfill your divine destiny and calling.

Providing yourself with this kind of accountability can save you from serious mistakes, but it could also guard you from being infected with sexually transmitted diseases that have critical and long-term consequences. A network of godly friends can help you stay on track with the Lord and assist you as you move forward to fulfill your divine destiny and calling.

Every one of us needs people to encourage us to fulfill the call God has placed on each one of our lives. In times of discouragement or temptation *not* to pursue our calling, these precious people can remind us of our destiny and help guide us back to the place where we can regain our momentum and begin making progress again toward the fulfillment of those dreams.

Accountability to godly people that the Lord places around you is part of His design for protecting your divine calling and your life. Having others to encourage you and speak the truth to you in love is a valuable gift not to be taken lightly. In fact, it is very difficult to maintain long-term spiritual and emotional health without people in your life who know you and who can help strengthen and fortify you in your Christian walk.

> Accountability to godly people that the Lord places around you is part of His design for protecting your divine calling and your life.

PANDEMIC DISEASES — THE IMPACT AND THE CURE

The violation of sexual laws prescribed in Scripture is having widespread consequences, resulting in the premature deaths of millions of people worldwide. As society throws its arms open to sexuality of every kind, it likewise opens itself wide to multiple diseases and tragedies that seem to have descended on the human race. For example, as discussed previously, mankind has been infiltrated with STIs as a result of ignoring God's unalterable laws. These diseases have spread to such an extent that from a natural standpoint, they cannot be contained.

I'm not saying that all disease is a result of an individual's sin or immoral behavior. However, diseases *that science knows* are spread through sexual contact will certainly continue to expand across all nations and all strata of society as the mindset of "anything goes" regarding sexuality continues to be established in that direction. But whether it's a growing pandemic of sexually transmitted diseases or superbugs that have infiltrated mass populations — believers need not fear these last-days "pestilences" foretold by Christ.

More than ever before, this is a time when we *must* live in obedience to the Word of God. When fear tries to attack our minds as we witness these emerging and reemerging diseases spreading among the human race, we must remember Exodus 15:26 (*NLT*), which says: "If you will listen carefully to the voice of the Lord your God and do what is right in his sight, obeying his commands and keeping all his decrees, then I will not make you suffer any of the diseases I sent on the Egyptians; for I am the Lord who heals you."

God is *for* you, not *against* you — and He will be faithful to His Word to deliver you from every evil attack of sickness. If you'll keep your heart pure before Him and maintain unwavering faith in His Word, protection and healing will be yours.

You would also do well to regularly meditate on the entire 91st Psalm. This psalm is filled with assurances of protection and deliverance from that which comes to ensnare, wreak havoc upon, and destroy.

> He that dwelleth in the secret place of the most High shall abide under the shadow of the Almighty. I will say of the Lord, He is my refuge and my fortress: my God; in him will I trust.
>
> Surely he shall deliver thee from the snare of the fowler, and from the noisome pestilence. He shall cover thee with

his feathers, and under his wings shalt thou trust: his truth shall be thy shield and buckler. Thou shalt not be afraid for the terror by night; nor for the arrow that flieth by day; Nor for the pestilence that walketh in darkness; nor for the destruction that wasteth at noonday.

A thousand shall fall at thy side, and ten thousand at thy right hand; but it shall not come nigh thee. Only with thine eyes shalt thou behold and see the reward of the wicked.

Because thou hast made the Lord, which is my refuge, even the most High, thy habitation; There shall no evil befall thee, neither shall any plague come nigh thy dwelling. For he shall give his angels charge over thee, to keep thee in all thy ways. They shall bear thee up in their hands, lest thou dash thy foot against a stone. Thou shalt tread upon the lion and adder: the young lion and the dragon shalt thou trample under feet.

Because he hath set his love upon me, therefore will I deliver him: I will set him on high, because he hath known my name. He shall call upon me, and I will answer him: I will be with him in trouble; I will deliver him, and honour him. With long life will I satisfy him, and shew him my salvation.

— Psalm 91:1-16

Living at the end of the age provides us ample opportunities to draw near to the Lord and to make Him our "refuge and habitation" (vv. 2,9). We need never fear *sickness, disease, pestilence,* or *plague*! The Lord is our protection as long as we are walking in obedience to His Word.

As we draw closer to the wrap-up of this period, we must learn to abide "under the shadow of the Almighty" for our protection and strength. We must embrace the Word of God in our studies and in our fellowship with Him in prayer. Our intimate fellowship with the Lord will position us to remain fearless and calm, confident that He is truly with us, guiding our every step.

Let's move on to the next sign in Matthew 24 that Jesus said we would see as we approach the end of the age. He prophesied there will be *earthquakes*, *fearful sights*, and *signs in the heavens* at the end of the age just before He returns, and that is what we will focus on in the next chapter.

Think About It

1. How did this chapter challenge you regarding God's healing provision and promises in the Bible? Has your desire increased to pursue a stronger walk of divine healing and health — and to bring healing in Christ's name to others who have been afflicted?

2. Do you see God's laws about morality in a new light after reading this chapter? Do you view those unalterable laws as His means of protecting physical lives and preserving families and generations? If yes, how so?

3. Consider making a commitment to memorize portions of the 91st Psalm and to meditate regularly on the entire psalm until its truth becomes real to you in your heart. Name some of the benefits to your walk with God if you were to walk true to that commitment?

Chapter Eight

Earthquakes, Fearful Sights, and Great Signs

Hollywood has produced movies about catastrophic volcano eruptions and mega-earthquakes so chilling that movie-goers regularly pack theaters to see these films. But is it possible that these scenarios are more than just the product of screenwriters' vivid imaginations? Could these theatrical catastrophes actually happen at some point in the future — and, if so, could that future time be nearer than we've considered?

If you think this is too fantastic to believe, remember that it wasn't so long ago — *in 2004* — that a violent underwater earthquake occurred in the Indian Ocean, off the coast of Sumatra in Indonesia, that literally shook the whole planet.[1] Several tsunamis were triggered as a result, raising the death toll to more than 225,000 people in 15 countries and making this cataclysm one of the deadliest natural disasters in world history.[2]

Some of the potential scenarios presented in this chapter may sound like speculation. But like the example in Indonesia, monumental catastrophic events in various parts of the world have collectively wiped out gigantic regions, displaced millions of people, and killed hundreds of thousands over the past 100 years. And we know that disasters of this sort will likely occur again.

WHAT JESUS SAID ABOUT EARTHQUAKES

As Jesus foretold events that would occur at the end of the age, He said there would be "…earthquakes, in divers places" (Matthew 24:7).

The word "earthquakes" in this verse comes from a Greek word that describes an *earthquake* or *seismic activity*. Because it is used in the *plural* form here, it emphatically tells us that Jesus was predicting a time of prolific seismic activity that will occur at the end of the age.

Luke recorded this same narrative about earthquakes in Luke 21:11. He wrote, "And great earthquakes shall be in divers places, and famines, and pestilences; and fearful sights and great signs shall there be from heaven."

The words "great earthquakes" in Greek literally mean *great seismic activity*. The word used in the original language can depict something *large* in size, or it can also mean *numerous* in quantity. Furthermore, Jesus stated that these earthquakes will occur in "divers places." This means the earth will be touched globally by increased seismic activity toward the end of the age.

Scientific record demonstrates that earthquakes are a part of the geological history of the earth. But Jesus was not giving a history of the earth when He spoke about earthquakes in Matthew 24:7 and Luke 21:11. He was forecasting *what will happen* in a condensed period of time at the very end of the era. According to Jesus, increased seismic activity will take place globally and a vast number of earthquakes will be felt in various places across the earth.

OUR EARTH IS TREMBLING

Recent reports made by the *United States Geological Survey* (USGS) estimate that several million earthquakes occur in the world each year.[3] However, many of these go undetected because they affect remote areas or register very small magnitudes. Because larger earthquakes have been so well-documented over the past 100 years — and their effect is more widespread — we know much more about greater earthquakes.

According to long-term records dating from about 1900, the USGS expects approximately 16 major earthquakes in any given year — 15 in the magnitude-7.0 range and 1 in the magnitude-8.0 range or greater. During the years 1973-2011, their records show those long-term averages were exceeded only 8 times: in 1976, 1990, 1995, 1999, 2007, 2009, 2010, and 2011.

The year with the largest total was 2010, with 24 earthquakes greater than or equal to magnitude 7.0. However, in other years in that 38-year span, totals were well below the 16-per-year number expected, based on long-term averages. For example, the year 1989 saw only 6 major earthquakes worldwide, and 1988 saw only 7 earthquakes.[4] But because scientists determine trends based on *many thousands of years* of data, their assertion is that the rate of these large earthquakes is relatively constant.[5]

Data on earthquakes has become readily accessible in recent decades, thus allowing the compilation of a more comprehensive global seismic record. Seismic waves are intricately recorded in real time across the globe using cutting-edge sensors, and the signals are processed with powerful computer technology.

These global seismic records reveal there are approximately 20,000 earthquake events each year. But due to gaps in coverage in remote and/or politically unstable regions, many small earthquakes go undetected. Extrapolating from the current global record, scientists are able to calculate that our planet is in fact probably experiencing several million very small earthquakes annually in the 2.0 and smaller range in magnitude.[6]

In the year 2012 alone, the annual number of earthquakes in the 2.0-2.9 range was estimated at 1,300,000.[7] In addition to these earthquakes, today's sophisticated technology also shows that there are currently an estimated 500,000 smaller tremors occurring each year and that they are shaking every corner of the earth.[8]

In Luke's gospel, Jesus said that there would be "great" seismic activity as the time of His return approached. We can infer from this verse of Scripture that "great" may mean *great quantity*. Approximately 500,000 smaller earthquakes are occurring every year. We know that even now, the earth is trembling with *great numbers* of earthquakes.

Although scientists are able to correctly record these cataclysmic events, they have no means of *predicting* them. However, they *can* calculate probabilities and project certain "likelihood" scenarios, based on long-term rates of occurrences and other data. As one ponders what scientists postulate *could* happen, a person could cower at the thought of a planet *unleashed* if it was not for the peace of God that He has made available for our hearts. But Jesus forecasted that earthquakes of great number around the globe would occur at the end of the age as a sign that the very last days were near.

> Approximately 500,000 smaller earthquakes are occurring every year. We know that even now, the earth is trembling with *great numbers* of earthquakes.

In Romans 8:22, Paul wrote, "For we know that the whole creation groaneth and travaileth in pain together until now." In light of the huge quantity of earthquakes that are occurring globally, is it possible that the earth is trembling and groaning as it prepares to give birth to the next age?

JESUS ALSO PREDICTED 'FEARFUL SIGHTS'

Luke's gospel added that at the end of the age, there would be "fearful sights [in the earth] and great signs shall there be from heaven" (Luke 21:11).

The words "fearful sights" are a mystery. This phrase comes from a Greek word that depicts *fright, horror*, or something that is *scary*. In fact, ancient Greek writers actually used this word to describe *monsters*, as these words conjure up horrific images and palpable feelings of dread and horror.

What Jesus was referring to in Luke 21:11 is not exactly clear, and Bible scholars cannot pinpoint what the words "fearful sights" entail. But whatever these words mean to a last-days society, Jesus said they would be "monstrous" in the eyes of God and the minds of men.

One possibility is that this phrase refers to some form of catastrophic natural disaster. However, it's interesting to note that when Jesus prophesied about the very end of the last days, He specifically listed several types of natural disasters by name, which might indicate that this additional warning of "fearful sights" refers to something else entirely.

One previously unimaginable possibility that has arisen in the modern age is the advent of a *horrific scientific or technological development.*

The idea that technology could unleash profound devastation comes as no surprise in the modern era. The Twentieth Century saw the first atomic bombs dropped at the close of World War II and the subsequent proliferation of nuclear weapons across the globe. Today many countries possess the means to wreak unthinkable devastation upon their enemies, and any such attack would have a profound impact on the fragile stability of the geopolitical system.

To date, no such attack has occurred since the U.S. atomic-bomb attack of Hiroshima and Nagasaki. However, rising geopolitical tensions have begun to erode this sense of safety — and many analysts speculate that the world could be closer to the brink of a nuclear catastrophe than at any time since the Cold War.

Certainly, the total destruction unleashed by a nuclear blast and the ensuing aftermath caused by radioactive fallout would classify as *horrific*, *monstrous*, and *scary*. Other possibilities exist as well. For example, virulent superbugs and weaponized chemical agents have been engineered at the behest of nations. Although kept under lock and key, the results would be catastrophic if a population was ever exposed to them.

> There are many different scenarios one could imagine that would fall under the umbrella of Jesus' warning of "fearful sights."

It's sufficient to say that there are many different scenarios one could imagine that would fall under the umbrella of Jesus' warning of "fearful sights." Any ideas will remain firmly in the realm of conjecture because Jesus purposefully kept this warning vague. However, one thing is certain — as a child of God, you do not need to fear these impending disasters.

'GREAT SIGNS FROM THE HEAVENS'

In Luke 21:11, Jesus continued His prophecy about the last days, adding, "...And great signs shall there be from heaven."

The Greek word for "great" in this verse describes something that can have a *mega* impact. It depicts something that has a *monumental, far-reaching*, and *deep* impact on the earth itself and its citizenry. Whatever these "great signs" are, they will appear "from heaven" — from the *heavens*, or sky — and it seems that much of the entire human race will be aware of them. When we see these signs, we should realize that we are on the precipice of something we've never encountered before.

Conjecture about the phrase "great signs from the heavens" can be endless. For example, some scientists suggest the possibility of solar flares with the capacity of short-circuiting electrical connections and communications — including completely shutting down the Internet — a cataclysmic event that would disrupt life on the entire planet.

Could the phrase "great signs from the heavens" be Jesus' way of prophetically speaking about a meteor or an asteroid that collides with the earth and creates vast destruction? Is it possible that "great signs from heaven" refers to nuclear bombs that descend from "heaven" and fall upon the planet? *Or could these signs be something beyond the scope of our present imagination?*

One thing is certain — the words Jesus chose in Luke 21:11 emphatically mean these "great signs" will descend *from* the heavens. In other words, before this age concludes, there will be some type of event, or series of events, descending *from the heavens* that will have a great impact on the population of the earth.

Luke 21:11 holds a mystery that Bible scholars and commentators haven't been able to explain. But what we do know with complete certainty is that "earthquakes, fearful sights, and great signs" *will* occur as we near the end of the age. Whatever these "fearful sights in the earth" and "great signs from heaven" are, the Bible tells us that they will be *horrific* and *monstrous* to those who experience them.

Once again, we see how imperative it is that we fill our hearts and minds with the Word of God in order to maintain peace in our lives. Only then can we be instruments of comfort, healing, and deliverance to a generation that will witness these calamitous events. This is not a time for us to cower in fear — *it's a time to be filled with the Spirit of God and to reach a generation that desperately needs the Good News of the Gospel.* This is truly our opportunity to rise and shine (*see* Isaiah 60:1)!

> This is not a time for us to cower in fear — *it's a time to be filled with the Spirit of God and to reach a generation that desperately needs the Good News of the Gospel.*

As we continue in the following chapter, we will see that Jesus prophesied the persecution and prosecution of Christians as precursors in the time just before He returns.

As you read, I believe you will be supernaturally strengthened and emboldened to maintain your stance on the Scriptures and your love for Christ. Take time to read the next pages slowly and digest the content that has been laid out for your information.

Think About It

1. Every word of God proves true (*see* Proverbs 30:5). This includes Jesus' words concerning the end of the age, about which He prophesied certain sights in "heaven and earth." What is your personal approach to what He said would surely come? Does it lean toward mere survival — or toward spiritual readiness to be a light and a witness for Christ as the end draws near?

2. What would you say to someone who is fearful about what Jesus foretold concerning manifestations in the earth's structure and in the sky just before He returned? If that individual is unsaved, you could lead him to salvation through Christ. If the person is saved, you could encourage him to "lift up his head" and look with joy for the final redemption that is to come (*see* Luke 21:28). Why not write from your heart the words that reflect what you would communicate to those who feel afraid?

Chapter Nine

Persecution

Let's continue Jesus' end-time discourse in Matthew 24:9 and 10, where He described signs that will be evident at the very end of the age. Jesus said, "...They shall deliver you up to be afflicted, and shall kill you: and ye shall be hated of all nations for my name's sake. And then shall many be offended, and shall betray one another, and shall hate one another."

In this passage, Jesus forecasted a time of persecution that would come to His followers. He said many would be *afflicted* and even *killed* — and that many would be *offended* and would *betray* and *hate* one another for the Gospel's sake. These various degrees of trouble inflicted on believers will come because of their ardent devotion to Christ and their refusal to bend to the current world trends.

> Various degrees of trouble inflicted on believers will come because of their ardent devotion to Christ and their refusal to bend to the current world trends.

I want us to look briefly at all five of these words — *afflicted, killed, offended, betrayed,* and *hated* — to see exactly what they mean in the Greek language. We're going to examine how these forecasts Jesus made had application in the past — throughout the centuries — and how they will have application again in the future.

Afflicted

The word "afflicted" in Matthew 24:9 is the Greek word *thlipsis*, which always describes *pressure, stress,* or *stressful situations*. We could say that *thlipsis* is a picture of one who feels trapped and unable to move, with so much pressure upon him that he is barely able to breathe. This word describes *pressure that is very difficult to bear*.

The word *thlipsis*, for example, could refer to pressure from family and friends, to hostile reactions from fellow workers, or to loss of employment due to one's faith. In other words, *thlipsis* pictures "event piled upon event" to cause a weight so heavy that it feels nearly *crushing*. It also depicts *bullying, harassment,* and *intimidation*. In extreme cases of this kind of pressure, or persecution, it could even mean *death*.

Early believers experienced harassments, arrests, imprisonments, and even deaths of the most gruesome types. It was pressure piled upon pressure as they were vigorously, sometimes *viciously*, persecuted. But Jesus used this word *thlipsis* to depict a persecution that will arise again at the end of the age.

Killed

The next word on our list is "killed" — translated from *apokteino*, a horrible Greek word that depicts *outright slaughter*. It pictures a person's life being viciously taken from him. Hence, by using this word "killed," Jesus was telling His disciples that many who followed Him would be killed — and some would die *terrible deaths*.

We know from history that this very definitely occurred, especially in the first three centuries of the Church. We know that it is happening again today in certain parts of the world where Christians are being executed — drowned, beaten, burned to death, beheaded, and so forth — for refusing to recant their faith in Christ. These are the faithful martyrs of the end-time Church.

Scandalized ('Offended')

As Jesus continued in Matthew 24:9 and 10, He also said that many would be "offended" — from the Greek word *skandalon* — and, yes, it is where we get our English word *scandal*.

The Christian faith was *scandalous* in the First Century, when believers lived by a solid biblical foundation in a tossing sea of philosophy that held no moral absolutes. Very similar to what is developing today, Christians were viewed as bigots and narrow-minded simpletons just for standing true to their faith.

Worst of all, from the perspective of the pagan society they lived in, early Christians would not acknowledge others' gods, but instead called Jesus the Lord over all. That meant Jesus was Lord over the countless gods and deities of that culture. In an early Roman world of paganism, that attitude was considered scandalous and unacceptable. Christians were viewed as a closed-minded, narrow-minded group, and their biblical views and beliefs were considered *offensive* during that period of time.

The Christian faith was *scandalous* in the First Century, when believers lived by a solid biblical foundation in a tossing sea of philosophy that held no moral absolutes. Very similar to what is developing today, Christians were viewed as bigots and narrow-minded simpletons just for standing true to their faith.

Betrayed

In Christ's list of words in Matthew 24:9 and 10, He also included the word "betrayed." As you will later see in Luke's gospel, Jesus predicted that acts of betrayal would be carried out even by members of one's own family.

BETRAYAL EVEN BY FAMILY AND FRIENDS

Jesus warned that believers would find themselves "betrayed" — translated from a word that means *to hand over* or *to deliver*. This "handing over" to authorities, or *betrayal*, by a believer's own family was certainly true at the Church's inception. Sadly, it's true even in today's world that the greatest resistance one experiences for his faith can often come from his own family.

Jesus elaborated in Luke 21, saying, "And ye shall be betrayed both by parents, and brethren, and kinsfolks, and friends; and some you shall they cause to be put to death. And ye shall be hated of all men for my name's sake" (vv. 16,17).

There is nothing more hurtful than betrayal from the hands of "parents, brethren, kinsfolks, and friends" (Luke 21:16). Yet Jesus said this would happen. It happened at the first of the Church Age, and it is happening now in places in the world where persecution is especially acute. In fact, in many parts of the world today, betrayal is so serious that, just as Jesus said, some are put to death.

This level of betrayal has not reached the shores of the United States of America; let's pray it never does. Nonetheless, as society becomes more progressive, biblical standards will be thrown to the wind more and more. And those who are uncommitted to the Word of God — or who have toxic feelings toward it — may oppose, even ruthlessly, those who remain "by the Book."

Hated

Jesus forecasted that Christians would be "hated" of all nations for His name's sake. The word for "hate" in Greek is *miseo*. This word describes *utter disgust* and *repulsion*. It is more than dislike; it is *pure hatred*. Jesus predicted that believers in various places and times would experience pure, undiluted hatred for His name's sake from the unbelieving world around them.

'THEY SHALL HUNT YOU'

When Luke recorded this part of Jesus' narrative about the end of the age, he recorded even more than what was recorded in Matthew 24:9,10. Luke wrote that Jesus said, "...They shall lay their hands on you, and persecute you, delivering you up to the synagogues, and into prisons, being brought before kings and rulers for my name's sake" (Luke 21:12).

The phrase "lay their hands on you" refers to *physical arrest*. The reason for the arrest is not specifically stated, but we do know it is for the sake of Jesus' name.

It is a fact that believers were *brutally arrested* in times past, and they are still being *brutally arrested* in time present. Jesus was prophesying that this *arresting* would also occur for His name's sake just before the end of the age when He returns for His Church.

It is a fact that believers were brutally arrested in times past, and they are still being brutally arrested in time present.

But Jesus didn't stop with physical arrest. He continued in Luke 21, saying, "...And [they shall] *persecute* you...."

Although the word "persecution" is not used in Matthew 24:9 and 10, Jesus used it in Luke 21:12 when He said, "...They shall

113

lay their hands on you, and *persecute* you, delivering you up to the synagogues, and into prisons, being brought before kings and rulers for my name's sake."

The word "persecute" in this verse is the Greek word *dioko*, and it depicts *one who vigorously pursues another*, as a focused hunter pursues an animal. In fact, *dioko* is a *hunting term*! In Luke 21:12, the word "persecute" could literally be translated, "They shall *hunt* you"!

Think about what this word is actually conveying. When a person hunts, he doesn't do it *accidentally*; he does it with *determination*. In fact, he does it so deliberately that he will vigorously pursue the tracks and scent of an animal until he apprehends or kills his game.

Persecution occurs when a very deliberate plan has been set in place to catch you — when someone has decided he will do all that is in his power to hunt you, trap you, seize you, and then deliver you to official authorities.

Jesus said concerning this strategic attack on the Christian faith, "...They shall lay their hands on you, and persecute you, *delivering* you up to the synagogues, and into prisons, being brought before kings and rulers for my name's sake" (Luke 21:12). This word "delivering" shows the treatment applied to the one being persecuted, and it pictures the person *handled with ill-treatment* and *handed over* to those in authority.

The word "deliver" actually means *to lead away as a prisoner or condemned man*. It was used in the Athenian language to depict an individual who was charged with a crime and delivered to the court for a trial. Although the word "synagogue" in this verse has a religious connotation, one must remember that synagogues were also places where court judgments were issued by Jewish officials to those found guilty of a crime. Hence, the word "synagogue" corresponds with the idea of *a court system*.

So in Luke 21:12, we find Christians *arrested, charged, and treated as guilty before a trial takes place* — and, finally, *brought in front of a court*.

According to Jesus in this verse of Scripture, once an official sentence of guilt has been pronounced, the accused are then taken "into prisons." The word "prisons" was translated from *phulakas*, which can refer either to a *jail* or a *prison* or to *some place of confinement* where one serves a sentence that has been rendered for his or her alleged offense.

What is the "crime" for the punishment Jesus was discussing here in verse 12? It is believers' commitment to remain true to Christ and His Word! Regardless of what society and the courts have declared to be the rule of the day, believers are called to hold fast to their internal convictions based on the Word. No matter what mounting pressure and affliction (*thlipsis*) may come, those who call Jesus Lord are never relieved of this divine requirement.

This "crime" of commitment to Jesus Christ is the same charge that was leveled against Christians in the first centuries of the Church. Those believers were largely immovable in their convictions, refusing to follow the spirit of their age. The result was harsh treatment from the governing powers, often involving legal prosecution and even death.

Jesus said in Luke 21:12 that believers would be brought before kings and rulers for His name's sake. The words "kings" and "rulers" (governors) refers to those invested with legal authority to make decisions and rulings regarding those who are brought before them. This shows the power of the government in the last days to inflict judgments upon those who will not comply with emerging societal standards — and with the laws enacted to enforce those standards.

SUPERNATURAL INSIGHTS AND ANSWERS

In Luke 21:13, Jesus continues, "And it [this situation of persecutions] shall turn to you for a testimony." The Greek could be interpreted, *"This will lead you to an opportunity to witness."*

In the early centuries of the Church, episodes of persecution brought Christians before kings, magistrates, and governors. Although the situations before them were grim, many were filled with the Holy Spirit and seized those opportunities to stand for Christ as witnesses for what He had done in their lives.

It's difficult to premeditate how one should answer in a moment of affliction and accusation. In fact, Jesus gave divine instruction in this matter when He said, "Settle it therefore in your hearts, not to meditate before what ye shall answer: For I will give you a mouth and wisdom, which all your adversaries shall not be able to gainsay nor resist" (Luke 21:14,15).

Jesus promises that if you are opposed or officially charged, your adversaries will not be able to "gainsay" or "resist" what the Holy Spirit puts in your mouth to speak.

This passage is one for you to claim for yourself! Jesus promises that if you are opposed or officially charged, your adversaries will not be able to "gainsay" or "resist" what the Holy Spirit puts in your mouth to speak.

The word "gainsay" is translated from a Greek word that means *to stand against, to withstand,* or *to resist.* The word "resist" is from a Greek word that means accusers will not be able to logically *refute* the words God puts in your mouth at that moment if you are accused or brought for judgment.

Just as the Holy Spirit was faithful to empower the Early Church in moments of prosecution and persecution, Jesus' promise remains the same to us today. If we find ourselves in places where adversaries are trying to corner us, accuse us, and charge us, we can rely on the Spirit of God. Jesus Himself said He would give us "...a mouth and wisdom, which all your adversaries shall not be able to gainsay nor resist" (v. 15). It is imperative that we develop an intimate relationship with the Holy Spirit and learn to lean upon Him in every situation we face.

When prosecution and persecution come to the Church at the close of the age, the Holy Spirit will be as faithful to us as He was to the saints who faced persecution at the inception of the Church. He will be the same faithful Holy Spirit who is right now strengthening and empowering Christians who are suffering all over the world. But we *must* make our fellowship with Him a priority so that we can know His voice, heed it, and be used as instruments He can speak through in times when His voice is so needed.

SERIOUS TIMES FOR CHRISTIANS WORLDWIDE

These are serious days. We cannot neglect the fact that approximately 75 percent of the world *right now* lives in situations that are precarious for believers.[1] *In fact, it is only a small fraction of the world that knows no Christian persecution.*

A part of this prophesied persecution was fulfilled in the early centuries when Christians endured intense attacks at the hands of various Roman emperors. But according to Jesus' prophetic predictions, the waves of persecution that struck the Church at its inception will attempt to slam against the Church again at the end of the age.

One reason why I have written this book is to prepare people for events that will occur just before Jesus returns. But I want you

> Be assured that in the midst of this period at the conclusion of the age, a mighty outpouring of God's Spirit will occur again before Christ returns for His Church.

to also be assured that in the midst of this period at the conclusion of the age, a mighty outpouring of God's Spirit will occur again before Christ returns for His Church. In fact, it will be the greatest outpouring of the Holy Spirit in the history of the Church, reserved specifically for these difficult and challenging times we are entering into.

It will be a different kind of outpouring than others have ever experienced because it will be the last great outpouring of this era. We do not know exactly how it will manifest, what it will look like, or how it will be experienced. But it will surely come — and as it does, we will know we are on the very brink of that long-awaited moment when Christ returns.

PERSECUTION, PAST AND PRESENT — 'BLASPHEMY' AS DEFINED BY THE RULING POWERS

Jesus devoted a significant amount of time to the persecution that His followers would experience in the future. His words came to pass as early as the second part of the First Century AD when persecution against believers was extraordinarily acute in cities across the Roman Empire.

It's important to point out that the primary charge against Christians in the early years could be summed up with the word "blasphemy." This is significant, especially in light of the legal charges being brought against believers in much of the persecuted world today.

First Century Christians were considered blasphemous for any number of reasons — all of which were determined by the evil ruling powers. Some of those reasons included: the failure to bow to the image of the reigning emperor; the refusal to enter pagan temples or recognize the authority of other gods; and the avoidance of pagan activities. This lack of participation with a depraved society was considered *blasphemous* in the pagan world of the Roman Empire.

It is interesting that today in parts of the world where Christian persecution is the worst, blasphemy is once again a primary charge leveled against believers. The same spirit that loomed over the Christian community in the First Century is overshadowing it once again.

Among a well-researched list of the top 50 countries where persecution is the worst — 39 of those countries are *Muslim*,[2] where the charge of blasphemy is often directed at Christian believers in order to "afflict" them.

Even in cultures not rooted in Islam, the First Century attitude that Christians were blasphemous is attempting to reemerge in society today. Although the world today is technologically advanced and sophisticated, certain elements that dominated the First Century — such as its diversity of beliefs, its ever-changing moral code, and its acceptance of moral perversion — are seeping back into the mainstream. These elements are encased within the noble-sounding ideas of *inclusivity* and *open-mindedness*. Many in positions of visibility and high esteem by the world's standards have "jumped on the bandwagon" in our day to promote these views.

But in our time and in the times to come, there is — and will continue to be — a remnant of believers who will not bow to the pressures of society, no matter how heavy those pressures become. Although some may collapse under the weight of these external forces, there are many committed Christians who will not bow to the new cultural norms of compromise, nor will they succumb to the pressures and afflictions that are forced upon them.

FAITH IN JEOPARDY

Although it has not completely occurred as yet, there is beginning to be a turn in society against those who stand for biblical moral absolutes. It is difficult to grasp the enormous scope of this turn. Nations that once thrived because of their adherence to biblical values have slipped into so much deception that the rule of the Christian faith is in jeopardy. This decline is the result of the "mystery of iniquity" at work, luring the world to a position of mutiny against God (*see* 2 Thessalonians 2:7) and grooming it for a new world leader — the antichrist.

> There is —
> and will continue
> to be — a remnant
> of believers who
> will not bow
> to the pressures
> of society, no
> matter how heavy
> those pressures
> become.

Using the power of the courts today, this progressive mindset is attempting to force Christians to comply with the spirit of this age. We are approaching a time most have never known in their lifetimes. Eventually, it is likely that those who refuse to cooperate with new state-sponsored regulations, especially about morality, will be subject to prosecution — a form of legalized persecution.

There's no way to get around it. The Bible prophesies that persecution in some form will come to the Church at the very end of the age — Jesus Himself said it would. It is time for the Christian community to be wide awake and united in order to spiritually withstand the powers of wickedness that will attempt to "modify" the Church and nullify its effectiveness in the last of the last days.

120

WHERE CHRISTIANS
ARE BEING PERSECUTED TODAY

Let me provide you the following information regarding modern-day persecution of the Church. I pray that what you read will awaken you to pray for the millions of Christians around the world who are *right now* being vigorously persecuted for their faith.

Christians are currently being persecuted in approximately 60 nations of the world.[3] This doesn't include recent court decisions "redefining" marriage, which will bring new pressures upon the American Church.

When I use the word "persecution" in this part of this chapter, I am using it based on a definition developed by Open Doors (**opendoorsusa.org**), an international mission organization that monitors persecution of believers worldwide. They state:

> Christian persecution is any hostility experienced from the world as a result of one's identification as a Christian. From verbal harassment to hostile feelings, attitudes and actions, Christians in areas with severe religious restrictions pay a heavy price for their faith. Beatings, physical torture, confinement, isolation, rape, severe punishment, imprisonment, slavery, discrimination in education and employment, and even death are just a few examples of the persecution they experience on a daily basis.

> According to the Pew Research Center, over 75 percent of the world's population lives in areas with severe religious restrictions (and many of these people are Christians). Also, according to the United States Department of State, Christians in more than 60 countries face persecution from their governments or surrounding neighbors simply because of their belief in Jesus Christ.[4]

The U.S. Department of State confirms this statistic that believers in more than 60 nations of the world face persecution because of their Christian faith.[5] Research by Open Doors reveals where in the world persecution is rated the very worst. Information also supplied by Voice of the Martyrs (**persecution.com**) helps us see how vast the problem of contemporary persecution of Christians really is.

Nearly four-fifths of the countries where persecution occurs is Muslim.[6] And as discussed previously, blasphemy is often the charge brought against non-Muslims in these nations, including Christians — just as it was in the early centuries of the Church until 313 AD.

As already noted, "blasphemy" is a far-reaching concept that can include what one believes all the way to what one wears. Its definition is interpreted differently by various regions and governments. Thus, with the charge of blasphemy, the door is thrown open to bring persecution against Christ's followers for a wide range of reasons — the "definition" of this word interpreted differently by each region and government where it occurs.

WHY CHRISTIANS ARE PERSECUTED

The following is a quote by the Open Doors organization about the perceived threat Christianity poses toward secular and religious ideologies in various parts of the world.

There are numerous reasons why Christians are persecuted. In some countries, severe abuse of Christians takes place under authoritarian governments. In the case of North Korea and other communist countries, authoritarian governments seek to control all religious thought and expression as part of a comprehensive plan to control all aspects of political and civic life. These governments regard some religious groups as enemies of the state because they hold religious beliefs that may challenge loyalty to the rulers.

Another reason why Christians are persecuted is hostility towards nontraditional and minority religious groups. For example, in Niger, more than 98 percent of the population is Islamic, and hostility comes more from society than from the government. Historically, Islam in West Africa has been moderate, but in the last 20 years, dozens of Islamic associations have emerged, which aim to restrict the freedom of 'deviant Muslims' (former Muslims who convert to Christ) and minority religious groups like Christians.

The lack of basic human rights is another significant part of persecution in some countries. For instance, in Eritrea, there are violations of the freedom of expression, assembly, and religious belief and movement, in addition to extrajudicial killings, enforced disappearances, extended detention, torture, and indefinite national service, which cause many Eritreans to flee the country.

Freedom of religion, like all freedoms of thought and expression, is inherent. Our beliefs help define who we are and serve as a foundation for what we contribute to our societies. However, today, many people live under governments that abuse or restrict freedom of religion. Christians in such areas suffer deeply, and are denied basic freedoms that humans should be entitled to.[7]

215 MILLION CHRISTIANS
ARE CURRENTLY SUFFERING

In 2016, the *Christian Post* online (**christianpost.com**) wrote, "The [Open Doors] 2016 'World Watch List' documents an unprecedented escalation of violence against Christians, making this past year the most violent and sustained attack on Christian faith in modern history. This research concluded that after the brutal persecution of Christians in 2014, [the year] 2015 proved to be even worse with the persecution continuing to increase, intensify and spread across the globe."[8]

Open Doors projects that approximately 215,000,000 Christians are suffering from some kind of persecution for their faith. That figure represents 1 in 12 believers worldwide.[9] By definition, these persecutions include harassments, pressures, hardness of life, and hostility — oftentimes violent and even leading to death — for calling oneself a Christian. Types of persecution range from pressure from family and community to government-imposed afflictions to violent acts carried out by terrorist groups.[10]

As we've already seen, Jesus foretold that "affliction" would come to believers in a last-days society. The word "affliction" depicts *pressures*, *harassments*, and *tortures*. Hence, it is clear that Christians are facing widespread persecution globally, including discrimination and violence at the hands of totalitarian regimes and hostile environments where faith in Christ is resisted and hated.

A "Religious Freedom in the World Report" in recent years stated that in more than half the countries of the world, religious freedom is curtailed. A survey conducted by journalists and scholars produced this finding and reported that in 116 of the world's nations (nations acknowledged by the United Nations and the U.S. Department of State) freedom of worship is obstructed to one degree or another, ranging from mild harassment and discrimination to outright persecution and violence.[11]

In 2015 the *Christian Post* online also published the following report on the status of Christian persecution in the world.[12]

Statistics on persecution of Christians vary.... The World Watch List, which ranks countries where Christians face the most persecution, has placed North Korea at number one for [more than] 13 consecutive years.

It is number one on the World Watch List, the most brutal and dangerous place in the world to be a Christian, because the government requires and enforces with hostility a total dedication to the hero worship of their leader....

Furthermore, Open Doors noted that Islamic extremism accounts for the main source of persecution in 40 of the top 50 countries ranked in the list....

Christian Solidarity Worldwide [**cswusa.org**] has also identified North Korea as one of the very worst places for Christians, especially in regard to its prison camps, where people can be sent for offenses such as owning a Bible.

"There is no freedom of thought, conscience, religion or belief, and any North Korean who expresses an opinion or a belief which differs from the regime's propaganda faces severe punishment. It is estimated that over 200,000 people are detained in prison camps in North Korea, where they endure dire living conditions and brutal torture. Many of these are Christians," CSW says on its website.[13]

'WHEN ONE MEMBER SUFFERS, WE ALL SUFFER' — HOW CAN WE HELP?

With growing resistance from neighbors, family members, local governments, opposing religious groups — including arrests, prosecutions, and even murders — Jesus' words about "affliction" in the last days is coming to pass before our very eyes. Think of it — potentially *215 million Christians* are facing affliction *right now*, simply because they have placed their faith in Christ.

This world of affliction seems so far removed from the peaceful communities where many of us live and freely go to the church of our choice. The persecution these fellow believers experience may seem too big for our minds to comprehend.

We need the Holy Spirit to open our hearts and minds to their reality so 1) we can pray fervently for our brothers and sisters in need; and 2) we can do whatever is possible from our side to help them in their tribulations.

How can you help? Perhaps you could financially contribute to a ministry that specializes in assisting believers caught in a wave of adversity because of their love for Christ.

While we leisurely purchase our morning coffee, go to lunch with our fellow workers, or enjoy an occasional movie — living relatively free of the threat of suffering — fellow believers are being *afflicted* because of their faith. What we spend freely and without much thought could make a difference in their ability to be defended, fed, or freed.

We must be conscious of our brothers and sisters and do what we can to sow into these precious lives — and the lives of those they will reach for Christ. We want to be able to look into Jesus' face one day and say, "Lord, we did what we could do to help."

THE TIMES IN WHICH WE LIVE

I must remind you again that the day the prophet Isaiah forewarned about is here — when what was once viewed as wrong by the culture has become right and *even celebrated* (*see* Isaiah 5:20). To speak or act in any way cross-grain to this new norm is now considered a symbol of injustice, bigotry, and intolerance.

These are the conditions of the final days of the age that Jesus spoke about in the Gospels — days in which we are designed by God to live in and to experience the triumphing power of Jesus Christ in the midst of storms (*see* 2 Corinthians 2:14). Some may succumb to the pressures of a changing society, but a remnant of power-filled believers — those who are yielded to the Holy Spirit — will stand. Those believers will experience the overcoming power of Christ!

Now let's turn to the next sign on the prophetic road to the end of the age. Jesus prophesied that there will be an emergence of *false prophets* as the age closes — false spiritual voices who will try to get the attention of the masses and distract them from the truth.

Some may succumb to the pressures of a changing society, but a remnant of power-filled believers — those who are yielded to the Holy Spirit — will stand. Those believers will experience the overcoming power of Christ!

Think About It

1. In times of intense pressure and persecution, Jesus Himself promised He would give you "...a mouth and wisdom, which all your adversaries shall not be able to gainsay nor resist" (Luke 21:15). How can you prepare, beginning right now, to participate with Christ in the fulfillment of this promise?

2. It's not enough just to know the voice of the Holy Spirit, especially in the very last days. You must heed what you hear, *acting* on what He says to you. How does your decision to fellowship with the Holy Spirit on a continual basis help you receive and act on His divine instruction?

3. Were you surprised to learn that believers in 75 percent of the world face precarious situations because of their faith? In what ways can you help your brothers and sisters in Christ who are being persecuted at various levels for their Christian beliefs?

Chapter Ten

False Religions

The first time I came in contact with a false religion, I was in my first semester at the university. I watched a group of young people wearing orange robes come dancing across my path on the main thoroughfare of the campus. The men had shaved heads, and they all danced about, chanting some kind of mantra, while they banged and clanged various drums.

As I watched this group of Hare Krishnas, my heart was saddened. I knew these were young people who were searching for truth, but they had been fed a lie. And because they had embraced it, they were in the grip of deception.

Attending college fresh out of high school was a real wake-up time for me when it came to false religions, for they seemed to *proliferate* among the students at the university. But a visit to the religion section of any major bookstore today will reveal that false religions and cults are big business — not just among young people, but among people of all ages.

Jesus prophesied that false religions would proliferate at the end of the age — and that is precisely what has happened in our time. Millions of people in the world today are being deceived in pseudo-religious movements.

CULTS AND RELIGIOUS MOVEMENTS

We've looked at several signs that Jesus enumerated in Matthew 24. So far, that list has included worldwide deception, wars and the threat of war, terrorism, racial and religious conflicts, uncivil politics, famine, hunger, manifold scarcities, diseases and plagues, earthquakes, fearful sights, signs in the sky, and the persecution, prosecution, and even martyring of Christians.

Jesus prophesied that false religions would proliferate at the end of the age — and that is precisely what has happened in our time. Millions of people in the world today are being deceived in pseudo-religious movements.

Then in Matthew 24:11, Jesus tells of yet another sign that would indicate we're approaching the very end of the age. He said, "*...Many* false prophets shall arise, and shall deceive *many.*"

In verse 11, the word "many" is the Greek word *polloi* — which tells us there will be *multitudes* of false prophets that will arise to deceive *multitudes* of people at the end of the age. There is no mitigating the word *polloi.* There is no other interpretation for this word. Christ was forecasting a deception that will affect *huge numbers* of people.

Jesus said, "...Many false prophets shall arise, and shall deceive many." The phrase "false prophets" comes from the Greek word *pseudoprophetes*, which is a compound of two words *pseudo* and *prophetes*. The word *pseudo* means *false*, and the word *prophetes* is the word for a *prophet*. Compounded into one word, the new word refers to a *pseudo-prophet* — a *false prophet* — or one who claims divine inspiration, but who is not sent by God. He or she asserts to speak by God-given revelation, but, in fact, that person is *pseudo*, or *false*.

In actuality, this *false one* may be speaking from a bona fide spiritual source, but it is a source other than God. Or perhaps the "prophet" is simply lying about his divine claims in order to form a religious following. Some of these men and women are deceived *themselves* and therefore deceive others who are under their leadership. Other leaders are intentionally deceptive with their assertions.

Regardless of the motive, these individuals are false and deceptive. And Jesus said there would be *polloi* — a *multitude* — of these false prophets who would "arise" in the very last days.

The word "arise" in Matthew 24:11 tells of a phenomenon when falsehood in religion will arise in the world in a notable way. False religions and cults have multiplied rapidly in these last times — each one presenting its own version of truth. Jesus said *many* of these types will appear on the scene at the very end of the age.

As I researched the list of false religions and cults that currently exist, I found that it was far too long to include the full list in this chapter. In fact, to deal at length with the subject of false religions and cults could be the theme of an entire book — and there are already some wonderful books written on this subject to help guide you.

The truth is that there are multitudes of individuals and religious organizations that claim to be divinely authorized and inspired. But they are *false* in that they do not represent the truth of the Bible. Some of them might preach and adhere to *some* Bible truth. But the core Bible doctrines of *salvation through Christ alone, His death and resurrection*, and *His present-day position and ministry* are tainted and erroneous — to the great detriment of the followers of these groups.

A few notable groups in this category that you would probably recognize are as follows:

- Baha'i Faith

- New Age religions

- Buddhism

- Scientology

- Hinduism

- Unitarianism

- Christian Science

- Islam

- Universalism (and Unitarian Universalism)

- Edgar Cayce organization (mysticism)

- Jehovah's Witnesses

- Mormonism

- Sun Myung Moon (Unification Movement/"Moonies")

- Eastern cults (Hare Krishna, etc.)

Each of these religious movements had an originator, or founder, who claimed some "special" visitation from God, whether by an angel, a dream, or some other supernatural means. He or she received so-called revelation that either does not exist within the Bible or that alters the meaning of the Bible.

Let's take a brief look at a few of the more well-known examples of modern-day false religions that began with a false prophet.

- Joseph Smith, founder of the Mormon movement, claimed to have had a divine visitation with an angel that resulted in the writing of an entirely different book of revelation, the Book of Mormon. Today there are millions of Mormons who spread the extra-biblical teachings of Joseph Smith. The claims of Smith continue to be proclaimed today through the mammoth-sized organization called the Church of Jesus Christ of Latter Day Saints.

- Christian Science, whose founder, Mary Baker Eddy, claimed divine inspiration and a new revelation about health and healing, which she claimed to have found *inside* the Bible. During her lifetime, she had hundreds of thousands of followers who followed her teachings on healing. Although Eddy has been dead many years, cities across America are dotted with Christian Science reading rooms where one can read and hear the erroneous, "supernaturally inspired" writings of Eddy.

- Edgar Cayce, the "sleeping prophet," was so called because he gave psychic readings to thousands of seekers while he was in an "unconscious" state. [1] His psychic activities drew a large group of followers who were completely dedicated to his claims of supernatural inspiration. Although he has been dead for decades, his organization continues with thousands of dedicated followers.

- Reverend Sun Myung Moon was the father of the worldwide Unification Church. Moon claimed to have had a supernatural visitation with Jesus, in which Jesus admitted to having failed His mission because He was killed on the Cross. According to Moon, Christ chose *him* to take His place and to create the family of God throughout the earth. This led to the formation of the Unification Church. Moon boldly referred to himself as the Prince of Peace and the Savior of the World. Hundreds of thousands of people around the world followed him through the years. Although Moon died in 2012, the Unification Church continues, so financially wealthy that it owns and operates a major newspaper and extensive properties across the United States.[2]

- The New Age movement is a conglomeration of all types of religions and spiritualist influences, filled with thousands of revelators, psychics, and mediums who claim to have tapped into some new stream of divine energy. It is a fact that *multitudes* — literally, millions of people — have been led in some form into the web of this great deception.[3]

The common denominator of the majority of false religions is they had a founder — a so-called prophet, seer, or leader. From the time of their respective supernatural experiences, these leaders began teaching their unique revelations to people who would blindly believe and follow them. Over the years, aggregated *millions* have pledged their allegiance — which has included the resources of their money and their time — to these cults and false leaders.

This has happened just as Jesus forecasted when He spoke to His disciples in Matthew 24:11. If you are amazed at the strange concoctions of partial truths, false religions, and cults that exist in the world today, just take these things as a sign that we are bumping into the end of the age! Jesus prophesied that such individuals and organizations would emerge in large numbers in the very last days.

It is happening just as Jesus foretold it.

There has never been a more important time in history for Christian believers to read, study, and meditate on the Word of God — the *Bible*. The way to circumvent spiritual seduction and deception is by knowing, understanding, and being rooted in the truth of God's Word. One key to ensuring rock-solid stability in an increasingly unstable world is by cultivating a heart of humility before God. He is looking for hearts that yearn for truth — spiritual reality as *He* sees it — and that embrace and submit to His Word as *absolute* truth.

> The way to circumvent spiritual seduction and deception is by knowing, understanding, and being rooted in the truth of God's Word.

The next sign Jesus foretold concerning the close of the age is very interesting and hits closer to home for most of us. Jesus prophesied that the increase of iniquity would cause the love of many to wax cold. *Are we seeing this sign in our world today?* Let's look to see.

Think About It

1. Do you know anyone who has been beguiled by a false religion? Did that individual at one time embrace the Bible as absolute truth, only to swerve from the path he or she once traveled? If so, what lessons can you learn from that person's life that will help you guard your own heart and your walk with God?

2. If you know someone who is involved in a false religion, will you commit to praying for that person so that the Holy Spirit can shine the light of truth on his or her heart and bring that individual into an understanding of God's Word?

Chapter Eleven

Iniquity Will Abound, and the Love of Many Will 'Wax Cold'

We've been looking at the signs of the end of the age and Christ's soon return that He enumerated for us in Matthew 24. So far, I've covered the larger topics of *mass deception, wars and rumors of wars, nations rising against nations and kingdoms against kingdoms, famines, pestilences, earthquakes, persecution,* and *false religions.*

Each one of the signs we've covered so far has the potential to affect thousands *and tens of thousands* of people at a time. But the sign I will cover in this chapter — "iniquity abounding and the love of many growing cold" (Matthew 24:12) — is singularly the sign that every one of us on the planet should pay particular attention to.

For example, a catastrophic earthquake could affect thousands and thousands of people in one part of the world while others in other parts of the world are not directly affected. Of course, the Bible says that when one member of the Body of Christ suffers, we are all affected, or *should be* affected (*see* 1 Corinthians 12:26). We must "weep with those who weep" and do all we can to lift up and come to the aid of fellow believers who are downtrodden or struck by catastrophe — whether it occurs from natural disasters, outbreaks of sickness and disease, scarcity and hunger, or persecution, etc. (*see* Romans 12:15).

Let's look at two more examples. When *pestilence* — a plague or infectious disease — strikes one portion of the population, that pestilence may have no direct effect whatsoever on the rest of the population. Also, short of a nuclear disaster that has the potential to destroy *massive* populations *worldwide*, even revolts and skirmishes — including terrorism — affect only certain numbers of people while other parts of the world live their lives relatively unchanged.

But this sign of *iniquity abounding with the love of many growing cold* can occur in every single home, church, community, city, state, and nation on earth. In fact, Jesus described this sign as a worldwide, societal occurrence. And because it will happen among "sinners and saints" across the board as the end draws near, Christians around the world are indeed susceptible to this mass phenomenon.

This chapter is perhaps the most critical chapter of the book for your life personally as a believer. I ask you to read and reread this chapter prayerfully as you seek to put down your roots deeper in Christ and to come up higher than you ever have before in your fellowship with God. I pray you are blessed and changed by what you read.

In this chapter, we will look at this important sign that will authenticate we are getting closer to the end of the age. Jesus said, "...Because iniquity shall abound, the love of many shall wax cold" (Matthew 24:12).

In Greek, the word "iniquity" actually describes *lawlessness*. A literal translation of this verse could be, "…Because *lawlessness* will abound, the love of many shall wax cold." The word "lawlessness" is *plural* in the Greek text, which tells us Jesus was foretelling a time when lawlessness would escalate around the world.

But what does *lawlessness* mean? The word "lawlessness" in this verse refers to the actions of an individual, a group of people, a nation — or even an entire society or culture — that has chosen to live apart from God's laws and principles. Although this person or group previously followed biblical laws and principles *in general*, they elected to forge their own ways of doing things that are *not* founded on the principles of God's Word. Thus, they are *lawless*, or living by their own newly evolving principles that are not based on established truths so vividly portrayed in Scripture.

A WORLDWIDE REJECTION OF GOD

In Romans 1, the apostle Paul wrote about a mass departure from God's principles and the results of such a fateful decision. In verse 28, Paul wrote, "And even as they [society] did not like to retain God in their knowledge, God gave them over to a reprobate mind, to do those things which are not convenient."

The word "retain" means *to hold* or *to embrace*, but in Romans 1:28, it is used to denote a people who have chosen *not* to hold or embrace the knowledge of God. Hence, they knowingly chose to "let go" of God and His well-established laws in order to go in a new direction.

The phrase "did not like to retain God in their knowledge" tells us that these people chose to let go of God and to lay aside the scriptures and principles that were once the foundation and guide for society. Romans 1:28 makes it clear that these people once had some knowledge of God, but elected to turn away from that knowledge and to go another way instead.

Instead of clinging to the spiritual laws and truths they had known — and that had guided them in the past — these people chose to go another direction.

This collective rejection of God and His time-tested truths is confirmed by Paul in Second Thessalonians 2:3, where he described a great "falling away" of people in the last days. Paul wrote, "Let no man deceive you by any means: for that day shall not come, except there come a *falling away* first, and that man of sin be revealed, the son of perdition."

In this verse, Paul prophetically described a falling away that will transpire in *society at large* at the very end of this age. In that hour, the "mystery of iniquity" (v. 7), which has been working for some 2,000 years, will be unleashed *full steam* in an attempt to lead the entire planet into various forms of deception. Once the Church has been "caught up" to meet the Lord in the air (*see* 1 Thessalonians 4:17), the lost world in general will reject God altogether and substitute Him with the son of perdition, otherwise known as the *antichrist*.

> Paul prophetically described a falling away that will transpire in *society at large* at the very end of this age.

But what about this "falling away" that will occur before all these events on the prophetic timeline unfold? The words "falling away" in Second Thessalonians 2:3 are used in the Greek Old Testament (Septuagint) to depict *a mass mutiny against authority.* But in this epistle to the Thessalonian church, they describe society revolting against the authority *of God Himself* at the conclusion of the age.

It is a fact that both Jesus and Paul prophesied that a great falling away *will* occur in the last days. The Bible describes it as a worldwide rebellion against God in society — across the planet.

DID GOD REALLY 'GIVE THEM UP'?

As a result of people's own choice to let God go from their consciences, Paul said that God "…gave them over to a reprobate mind, to do those things which are not convenient" (Romans 1:28).

We must ask ourselves this question concerning those who "fall away," choosing not to "retain God in their knowledge": Was it the Lord who gave *them* up — or did they turn from God and give up their knowledge of *Him*?

In this verse, the Greek language makes it clear that God did not "walk away" and abandon them, as some suggest. Instead, He responded to *their own desire* and released them to follow their wayward instincts. When He did, Romans 1:28 also reveals that they became "reprobate" in their thinking.

'REPROBATE' — A SIN-DAMAGED MIND

The Greek word for "reprobate" depicts a mind that no longer thinks or reasons correctly. Due to the influence of sin, it has become *unfit*. Although the words *twisted* or *perverted* are uncomfortable to use in today's world, these are actually the correct words to depict a reprobate mind. It is a mind that is damaged as a result of sin or of a drifting away from God's authority.

> The Greek word for "reprobate" depicts a mind that no longer thinks or reasons correctly. Due to the influence of sin, it has become *unfit*.

The word "reprobate" thus pictures the mind of an individual, or even the mind of

141

an entire society or culture, becoming ill-affected and sin-damaged, especially in regard to conclusions about moral issues. Possessing such a mind, especially concerning issues of morality, leads to reprobate behavior as one eventually begins to conform his actions to what he believes. A reprobate mind will eventually produce reprobate behaviors.

A reprobate mind is one that has become so distorted that it eventually loses its ability to discern what is morally right and wrong. Although that mind may remain brilliantly intellectual in many respects — morally, it has become debased. In God's view, it is a mind that has lost its ability to separate good from evil and to sense what is right and wrong.

> *A reprobate mind is one that has become so distorted that it eventually loses its ability to discern what is morally right and wrong.*

As a result of having sin-damaged minds, these people "...do those things which are not convenient" (Romans 1:28). This is an example of how reprobate thinking eventually produces reprobate behaviors. Notice the words "not convenient." In Greek, it actually means *not morally right or fitting*. A reprobate mind eventually loses the ability to discern right and wrong, even to the point of justifying wrong as right and evil as good — and, *conversely*, justifying right as wrong and good as evil (*see* Isaiah 5:20).

This dilemma of moral confusion is precisely what Jesus was referring to in Matthew 24:12 when He said that iniquity, or *lawlessness*, will abound in society as we collide against the very end of the age.

This prophecy not only applies to a lost world, but the word "reprobate" can also refer to those in the Christian community who have veered from the truths of God's Word. They have made so many exceptions for sinful behavior that it has produced in them a mind that no longer feels the pain or conviction of sin. Behaviors that once grieved and broke the heart are now being done with no feeling of pain to the conscience whatsoever.

IS THERE HOPE AND A CURE?

For believers who have made the mistake of yielding to sinful behavior for so long that it has spiritually damaged their hearts and minds, there is *hope*. If they will acknowledge that they've strayed and are willing to repent (*see* 1 John 1:9), the Holy Spirit will rise up as a mighty force within and begin to invade their willing minds to renew them again to the truth.

> For believers who have made the mistake of yielding to sinful behavior for so long that it has spiritually damaged their hearts and minds, there is *hope*.

This is a transformation of the mind that will require one to *submit* his or her mind to the Word of God and the work of the Holy Spirit (*see* Romans 12:1,2). It will require courage and commitment, for once the mind has become reprobate, it can only be restored to its previous condition by submitting itself 100 percent to the truth of God's Word.

It is simply a fact that once a mind has become *debased*, it takes a great commitment to renew it. But the good news is that if a wayward believer is willing to turn, the Holy Spirit will do the miracle, renewing that sin-damaged mind to a right, holy, fit condition!

HEARTS HARDENING
AND LOVE GROWING COLD

Jesus said, "...Iniquity [lawlessness] shall *abound*..." (Matthew 24:12). That word "abound" is from a Greek word that means to *increase, flourish,* and *overflow.* We know, of course, that Jesus was speaking of a worldwide condition in the very last of the last days.

From a sociological standpoint, this word was originally used to depict *masses of people,* so this context indicates *masses that lack moral understanding.* The word "masses" presents the right idea, for this "abounding iniquity" that Christ spoke of is a state of affairs that is and will be developing worldwide, not just in one part of the world. As this occurs, lawlessness and a lack of moral understanding will abound among the masses — and society will slide further and further into rebellion against God.

The "mystery of iniquity," which I referred to in Second Thessalonians 2:7, is at work to groom society for this condition of lawlessness, the worldwide rejection of God, and the introduction of the "son of perdition" after the rapture of the Church (*see* 1 Thessalonians 4:17). That is where this "mystery of iniquity" has set its sights, and this is why the world seems to be *rushing* through such tumultuous changes as we come to the close of this prophetic season. As stated at the first of this chapter, iniquity — *lawlessness* — will *flourish* at the end of this age and will seem like a river spilling over its banks.

In Matthew 24:12, Jesus was prophesying of a time that would come when immoral *thinking, believing,* and *acting* would affect nearly every facet of society. It will be a time of great moral confusion that leads to widespread immoral behaviors.

In Matthew 24:37 and 38, Jesus specifically describes a last-days society as "the days of Noah." Noah's day — the time before the Flood — was a time when immoral behaviors were prevalent in the world. And it wasn't just a few who were affected in that climate of overflowing iniquity and lawlessness. The entire population of that time was morally affected — and Jesus foretold that as we entered the wrap-up of the last age, it would once again be as the days of Noah. Only those who draw close to Jesus will avoid the defilement of this period. An on-fire, committed remnant that fixes their eyes and their hearts on Jesus will avoid the moral debasement that will occur throughout a last-days society.

Just look at the world around you. We are in the midst of a morality-altering period. Moral filth and violence are overflowing through every avenue and medium — television, movies, music, Internet, gaming, print, and even educational institutions. Man's mind, marvelously created by God, is being damaged by sin — and our youngest members of society are the most vulnerable.

> An on-fire, committed remnant that fixes their eyes and their hearts on Jesus will avoid the moral debasement that will occur throughout a last-days society.

THE PROCESS OF GROWING COLD

Jesus continued in Matthew 24:12, saying, "And because iniquity shall abound, the love of many shall wax cold."

According to Jesus, one consequence of lawlessness is growing cold toward God and toward others. It is important to note that Jesus said, "…The love of *many* shall wax cold."

The word "many" in Greek means *multitudes*. Jesus wasn't describing something that would affect only a few people here and there. This "waxing cold" could impact the greater part of mankind, even many in the Church. Those who are affected inside the Church will lose their sensitivity to the Holy Spirit's guidance and dealings — which will likely affect their view of right and wrong and corrupt the purity of their moral standards.

We as believers have a responsibility in this hour to delve into the Word and seek Him with fervor as never before. It is necessary to remain sensitive to the Holy Spirit so that our own love doesn't "wax cold." Despite the strong sway of the world and its trappings, nothing in life is more exciting than walking with God! There is nothing more satisfying than finding and fulfilling our place in His master plan in the time that remains before Christ returns.

WHAT IT MEANS TO BE 'PAST FEELING'

The apostle Paul also alluded to the issue of mind-damaging sin and iniquity when he wrote by the inspiration of the Holy Spirit, "Who being *past feeling* have given themselves over unto lasciviousness, to work all uncleanness with greediness" (Ephesians 4:19).

What does it mean to be "past feeling"? I'll illustrate it for you using a story from my childhood.

When I was a young boy in school just learning to write, I would press so hard on my pencil that I formed a callus that is still on my finger today. By *pressing, pressing, pressing* the pencil onto the paper as I formed each curve and stroke, I also pressed the pencil into my finger. I made that spot so thick and calloused that even now, I have no feeling there whatsoever. I could stick a pin into that part of my finger and feel absolutely nothing.

This is precisely what happens when a Christian commits sin again and again and again. He eventually grows calloused to that sin, and he no longer feels the pain that it once produced in his heart. Instead, he adapts to the callousness and learns to live in sin in that area of his life with no feeling about his wrongdoing.

This condition of becoming calloused in some area occurs when a person participates in sin or dwells on thoughts of sin again and again. At first, the sin pricks his conscience. But if he continues to yield to the temptation and routinely "apply the pressure" of that sin against his heart and soul, he will harden himself — just as I hardened that spot on my finger through pressure until it formed a callus. That person will begin adapting his beliefs and opinions to that sin until he no longer feels the pain of conviction that was once produced by his wrongdoing.

There are people who have tolerated sin or sinful thoughts so long that they have lost the ability to feel conviction in that area of their lives. This is why it is vital that all preaching and teaching is Word-based and precise, anointed, and straightforward. Only that kind of preaching and teaching has the power to shake people from slumber and keep them tender of heart, yet strong in spirit.

THE PULPIT'S COMPLETE TASK

Let's look at what preaching and teaching does for the heart and soul of the hearer when it is done in the power of the Holy Spirit.

I certainly would not include all pastors, preachers, and churches in the statement I'm about to make — but it is a fact that much preaching and teaching in pulpits has changed in these last times. Much of what is heard in pulpits today is more *motivational* than *scriptural*, with the emphasis on living improved lives versus loving God and hating sin — which, by the way, is God's way of achieving an improved life!

The apostle Paul clearly said that Holy Spirit-inspired preaching should do three things: *reprove, rebuke,* and *exhort* (*see* 2 Timothy 4:2). Therefore, if all a congregation hears is *exhortation* — which can rightly include motivation-based messages — it means two-thirds of what preaching is supposed to do is completely left out!

Spirit-inspired preaching should do all three: *reprove, rebuke,* and *exhort.*

We all have to continually keep ourselves stirred up to avoid spiritual complacency. As I said, good Bible preaching and Spirit-empowered expository teaching shakes people from apathy and keeps them strong. Hence, it is essential that we have all three aspects of the preaching of the Word in our pulpits — *reproving, rebuking,* and *exhorting.*

Let me explain the difference between these three facets of the ministry of the Word from Second Timothy 4:2. Paul commanded us as ministers of the Gospel: "Preach the word; be instant in season, out of season; reprove, rebuke, exhort with all long suffering and doctrine."

- "Reprove" is from the Greek word *elegcho.* In this context, it means *to convict or to censure a listener* with the clear preaching and teaching of the Word of God. To reprove is to convict with such effectual feeling that one is brought to his senses and to the point of conviction for wrong actions and wrong thinking in his life. The offender must choose either to repent or to reject what he now knows to be true. This is a supernatural work of the Holy Spirit to bring change to a person's heart, but it requires a personal response from the listener in order to effect a change.

  "Reproving" is an essential part of preaching and teaching in order for the Holy Spirit to produce purity and spiritual fire in the Church!

- "Rebuke" is from the Greek word *epitimao.* It is the same word that is used in the gospels when Jesus "rebukes" a demon spirit. It is *a sharp correction that expresses strong disapproval of one's thoughts, actions, or deeds.* It points out where an offender is wrong and gives him instruction on how to do what is right. It represses the prevalence of evil and strongly opposes what is wrong in a person or in society.

  It is essential for sin and sinful behavior to be "rebuked" by those in the pulpit at the right time and the right setting, as led by the Spirit of God. For a pastor to ignore sin and never address it permits a congregation to avoid taking the issue of sin seriously. The absence of godly rebuke can even lead believers to become calloused to sin and its ravaging consequences.

- "Exhort" is from the Greek word *parakaleo*. It means *to urge, to exhort,* or *to admonish.* It is a type of preaching or teaching that undergirds believers with spiritual strength and admonishes them to press forward toward God's highest will, regardless of the opposition faced along the way. Godly exhortation is strong, anointed, and motivational, stirring the listener to cast off defeat and press on toward victory.

  This kind of preaching and teaching is essential to keep the Church focused on victorious living and the fact that they can overcome the world and achieve every dream God has put in their hearts.

All three of these elements of God's Word must be practiced in the Church. Unfortunately, the first two — *reproving* and *rebuking* — have largely been put aside, lest people be offended. As a result, the deeper issues of the heart that need to be addressed and corrected — *which are so vitally important* — are often being ignored. This is not always the case, but it's true that most preaching and teaching today consists of *exhortation* to stir the saints with a positive message. Although this type of preaching is good, it leaves out the other two vital elements that are so essential for people's hearts to be convicted and changed by the power of the Holy Spirit.

Let me be clear: To be accurate and obedient to the call of God as ministers of the Gospel, we *must* reprove, rebuke, and exhort — and we must do it with "all long suffering and doctrine" (*see* 2 Timothy 4:2).

The word "longsuffering" is the Greek word *makrothumia*, which is a compound of the words *makros* and *thumos*. The word *makros* indicates something that is *distant, far,* or of *long duration.* The word *thumos* means *anger,* but it also embodies the idea of *swelling emotions* or *a strong and growing passion about something.*

Makrothumia can also be translated as the words *forbearance* and *patience.* It is like a candle that has a very long wick and is therefore prepared to burn a long time. It is ready to forbear and patiently wait until someone finally comes around and *makes progress, changes,* or *hears* what you are trying to communicate or teach him or her.

Preaching and teaching "with all long suffering" means that we who preach must do it *over and over again* until the message preached is understood, embraced, and brings about life transformation. There will *never* be a time when reproving, rebuking, and exhorting will not be needed in the Church. Hence, we must study and equip ourselves as ministers to continually bring these three elements of God's Word to His people.

Unfortunately, often when a minister skillfully and compassionately "reproves and rebukes" in obedience to God's charge on his life, he is vilified as being critical and negative. In *some* cases, the ministers themselves are bullied and abused by congregations for fulfilling this commandment of God to "preach the Word, reproving, rebuking, and exhorting *with all long suffering and doctrine"* (*see* 2 Timothy 4:2). But God's commandment doesn't change. He charges His ministers to preach the Word without compromise, regardless of the consequences.

WHAT IT ACTUALLY MEANS TO 'WAX COLD'

We've read Jesus' words that in the last days, "...Because iniquity shall abound, the love of many shall wax cold" (Matthew 24:12).

The words "wax cold" are a translation of a Greek word that means *to progressively become cold-hearted*. It depicts people who have become numbed — perhaps by personal sin, by the condoning of sin in others, or by a sinful environment. Perhaps they have become cold spiritually by allowing the moral changes in the world around them to negatively affect their own standards. The lawlessness that abounds more and more may have rubbed off on them as well.

To maintain our fire for Jesus in these last times, we must choose to withdraw from ungodly influences that numb us to the consequences of sin. It is essential that we stay close to the fire of the Spirit if we're going to stay passionate in our love for Jesus. If we make any other choice, we run the risk of allowing the lawlessness that is running amuck in the world to affect us, and just as Jesus said, our love will grow cold. So let us purposefully draw near to the fire of the Spirit. Jesus is coming soon, and when He comes to evacuate the Church from planet Earth, we do not want Him to find that we have "waxed cold" and grown disinterested in the faith.

> To maintain our fire for Jesus in these last times, we must choose to withdraw from ungodly influences that numb us to the consequences of sin.

Let's proceed to the next chapter — where, *finally*, we will discover the ULTIMATE SIGN that Jesus declared we would see just before He returns for His Church. Jesus listed many signs along the end-time prophetic road, but He specifically stated that when we see this one final sign, we can know with *assurance* that this age is closing and He is about to return!

Think About It

1. Contemplate how this end-times sign of *iniquity abounding and love growing cold* can potentially affect every person on the planet? What must Christians do to avoid falling into this category of last-days believers?

2. Consider all that's required for a person to lose 100 pounds of excess weight. Compare that grueling process with the strenuous practice of "re-bending" one's reprobate mind to think once again in line with the Bible. What do the two processes have in common? Which is easier — the process of *maintaining* a desired condition or *correcting* a dangerous condition that developed from disobedience and neglect?

3. Can you think of a time when a loving rebuke or reproof from your pastor steadied your course or kept you from seriously erring from your God-directed path? If so, was your heart more tender and your fellowship with the Lord sweeter as a result? Take a moment to ponder your possible spiritual condition had you *not* received that loving redress.

Chapter Twelve

'And Then the End Will Come': The Final Sign Just Before Jesus Comes!

We finally come to the *ultimate* sign that Jesus Himself gave to indicate we've arrived at the *very end* of the age. In Matthew 24:14, He said, "And this gospel of the kingdom shall be preached in all the world for a witness unto all nations; *and then the end shall come.*"

When Jesus gave this Great Commission to His apostles and to others who followed Him, it was truly an enormous assignment. Fulfilling this charge to "preach the Gospel of the Kingdom" would require them to travel by land — often on foot — and by sea to reach every part of the then-known world. Apostles and believers, empowered by the Spirit of God, traveled far and wide to preach the message of the Kingdom. But even with their passion and commitment to reach their world, it was not possible for them to reach the *whole* world of their time.

It is actually astounding how far Christ's followers journeyed to preach the message of the Kingdom, yet the world was bigger than they were able to reach in their lifetime. I encourage you to read my book *A Light in Darkness, Volume One* [1] to see just how far the apostles traveled in their efforts to obey the Great Commission. You will find these pages to be remarkable as you consider the time in which they lived and learn how much land they traversed to fulfill this command of Jesus.

But in our own lifetime — due to the development and evolution of technology — it *is* possible to reach *the entire planet* in one way or another with the message of the Gospel. The prophet Daniel prophesied that in the end of days, "...many shall run to and fro, and knowledge shall be increased" (Daniel 12:4).

Certainly we are living in a day when worldwide travel has become commonplace, and missions travel has increased as a result. Also, knowledge and technology have increased as never before in a very short period of time. These developments are all being used in the last days for the preaching of the Kingdom of God to fulfill the Great Commission, which Jesus gave to the Church (*see* Matthew 24:14; Mark 16:15-18).

If someone has access to a mobile phone today, he has potential access to the preaching, teaching, and the declaration of the Gospel. If that person doesn't have a smart phone, but has a television, radio, or access to the Internet through a computer or some other recently developed device, he most likely possesses accessibility to the Gospel in some form.

WE'RE ALMOST THERE

Jesus was referring to the propagation of the Gospel at this magnitude when He said, "And this gospel of the kingdom shall be preached in all the world for a witness unto all nations: and *then* the end shall come" (Matthew 24:14).

It has become nearly possible for the *whole world* to hear the message of the Gospel and the Kingdom of God — and to even hear it in many languages. As fast as the Internet is spreading across the globe, it won't be long until the whole world will be interconnected — with the possibility of reaching every people group.

According to Jesus, the *last, greatest,* and *final* sign that we are at the very end of this present age is that the Gospel will be preached in all the world for a witness to the nations. Once this moment is reached, this present era will end as the Rapture occurs and the Church is evacuated from the earth.

> According to Jesus, the *last, greatest,* and *final* sign that we are at the very end of this present age is that the Gospel will be preached in all the world for a witness to the nations. Once this moment is reached, this present era will end as the Rapture occurs and the Church is evacuated from the earth.

THE GOSPEL PREACHED IN ALL THE WORLD

Jesus said, "...This gospel of the kingdom shall be preached in all the world..." (Matthew 24:14).

The word "preached" is a form of the Greek word *kerux*, which depicts one or many who "preach" the Word of God. The word "world" is translated from the Greek word *oikoumene*. It is a compound of *oikos*, meaning *a house*, and *meno*, which means *to stay, abide,* or *inhabit.* Compounded as one word, *oikoumene* in this phrase "in all the world" describes *the inhabited world* where people live in cities, towns, and villages — in various types of homes — all over the earth.

In other words, this Gospel of the Kingdom will be potentially heard wherever people live and dwell all over the world!

Jesus also said the Gospel will be preached for a "witness" — the Greek word *marturion*. This word depicts *a witness who stood in a court of law*. It also refers to *those who might possibly bear the brunt of being faithful to what they have proclaimed*.

Those who bore "witness" in a court of law in ancient times realized that they could later risk the brunt of persecution for speaking the truth. Likewise, Jesus foretold that in the last of the last days, there could be ramifications for being a witness to the truth. This dovetails with what we studied in Chapter Nine, where we saw that approximately 215,000,000 Christians per year are being hassled, bullied, and seriously *persecuted* for their faith — some persecuted to the point of death because of the truth they bear witness to.

Jesus said, "And this gospel of the kingdom shall be preached in all the world for a witness unto all *nations*...." The word "nations" is the Greek word *ethnos*, which could be translated as *nations* or *ethnic groups*. In this verse, Christ proclaimed that at the very end of the age, the Gospel will be proclaimed to every nation and every ethnic group.

Since this is the case, we must consider how many unreached nations and ethnic groups have yet to hear the Gospel. How will this miracle occur — that each nation and group will be penetrated with the message of the Gospel in such a short time as we come to the end of the age?

THE GOSPEL'S GLOBAL IMPACT THEN AND NOW

In previous centuries, when missionaries started the arduous journey to their foreign-mission destination, they often packed their belongings in the casket they planned to be buried in. Most knew that it was unlikely they would ever return to their native soil.

But today the proclamation of the Gospel is much different. Some ministers still pay the ultimate price of their lives to fulfill their heavenly assignments. But largely, heralding the Gospel is carried out through safer means. Airplane travel makes going from location to location more convenient. Medications are also more readily available. And so much of the Gospel is delivered by various media instead of only "in person."

I think of my own ministry. Although we regularly do ministry face-to-face — and there is no replacement for that type of personal ministry — it is also true that for decades we have been broadcasting the teaching of God's Word over television and the Internet. Yes, we have conducted many massive crusades in which we have seen the lost saved and the sick healed. We have started churches, and we pastor a large church in Moscow right now. But much of our outreach has been through new and modern vehicles of communication. Every week, I reach thousands of people through text messages, by phone, and through TV programs that are seen via terrestrial stations, satellite stations, and the Internet.

With all these amazing technological advances available for proclaiming the Gospel, there is still an enormous number of unreached nations and people groups that have never heard the Good News of Jesus Christ. Yet against that challenging backdrop, Jesus' words in Matthew 24:14 still ring true: The end of this present age will come when the entire *inhabited world* has had an opportunity to hear the message of the Gospel!

Jesus said the *availability* of the Gospel would be possible for every nation and ethnic group at the end of the age. Of course, these "availing of opportunities" will occur through the burgeoning growth of media. All forms of media will carry the message to people who have never had a chance to hear it before!

Jesus explicitly stated that when this happens, "... *Then* shall the end come" (v. 14).

The word "then" is very specific, and in the Greek language, and it points to an exact time. So when the Gospel is being communicated through airwaves, Internet connections, and sundry other means, "then" — at that moment — the end can potentially come.

The word "end" is the Greek word *telos*, which describes the *completion* of a thing. This no doubt means that the *completion* of the very last days will occur when the Gospel message has been made available to *every nation* and *every ethnic group* on the face of the earth. When the Gospel's penetration has occurred in every inhabited place on earth so that all have the ability and opportunity to hear, *then* the *end* — the completion of the age — will come.

There is no question that with the rapid advances being made in technology, this condition of the widespread availability of the Gospel in every place will happen within our lifetime. Once the Gospel becomes available in every place, the conditions will be *finally, exactly* right for His return to "catch away" His Church (*see* 1 Thessalonians 4:17). In other words, once the Gospel has reached every people group, Christ's return could happen at *any* time!

HOW MANY PEOPLE GROUPS
HAVE NEVER HEARD THE GOSPEL?

This raises the question of how many people in the inhabited world have never had an opportunity to hear anything about the Gospel of Christ. At the time of this writing, there are approximately 7,078 unreached people groups, amounting to about 3.14 billion people who have never heard the Gospel of Jesus Christ.[2]

Even if millions and millions of the 3.14 billion people yet unreached ultimately *reject* the salvation message, we must at least see to it that they have an opportunity to receive or reject it. *This is our God-given responsibility as commissioned by Christ to His Church.*

With all the advances being made in more sophisticated technology, this realization could happen very quickly. We are not so far from being able to address every nation and ethnic group with the Gospel — *in their own languages.* Also, because the use of the English language has increased in many places across the world, it is becoming less necessary for people to hear the salvation message in their native tongue.

I was recently in a *very* remote part of Asia visiting an "unreached" people group. Life there is primitive. Yet I must tell you that I was shocked at the number of sophisticated mobile phones that existed in that particular area. I don't know if those people listen to the Gospel messages on their devices, but the *possibility* of it certainly exists for them. The fulfillment of Jesus' prophecy where that people group is concerned has already come.

As I travel to remote regions of the earth, I am always stunned to see the mobile phones being carried by those I never dreamed would possess one. With one hand, they push a plow with an ox — and with the other hand, they hold a cell phone! Through this type of digital and cellular technology, the *possibility* of the Gospel reaching these approximate 7,078 unreached groups is already nearing completion. People may refuse to listen, but they will have the Gospel message *available* to them nevertheless.

There are approximately 4,770,000,000 mobile phones in the world right now[3] — *almost 5 billion phones* — many of which have the possibility for Internet connections. Considering the population of the earth is about 7.6 billion at the time of this writing,[4] this could mean that almost 63 percent of the world's population has a mobile phone. Since smart phones have become so prominent, it is reasonable to conclude that Christian programming is available to most of this large percentage of people *if* they choose to watch or listen to it.

What's even more amazing to me is that there are thousands of TV channels in the world today that have the potential to carry Christian broadcasting in nearly every "tongue" of the world, which is about 7,100 languages.[5] These stations are airing programming to approximately 1.6 billion connected television sets in 1.57 billion households.[6] Some of those households are in very remote parts of the world. These figures don't even include the inestimable number of shortwave radios owned by people all over the planet! Thus, it is easy to see that Christian programming is at least *potentially* available right now in many of these places.

Although there are approximately 3.14 billion people on the earth who have never heard the Good News of Jesus Christ, the Gospel message is having a worldwide impact and is penetrating thousands of these unreached people groups via communications technology. *This means the end of this age is very near!*

WHAT GRIEVES THE HEART OF GOD

At this time, it is essential that we put forth our best efforts to reach the unreached. Especially at the end of this age, we must not forsake our ardent support of *foreign missions* in places where people are as yet untaught or the name of Jesus is not yet known. We must give sacrificially at this time in history to *especially* reach the nations and ethnic groups that have never heard the name of Jesus.

Unfortunately, we are living in a time when passion for the lost is waning. Many pulpits never deliver messages on Heaven or hell — and don't even give invitations for the lost to be saved in their own churches. This makes it no surprise that there has been a decrease among churches that give to foreign missions.

Every one of us will have to answer to Jesus for the way we steward the money that comes into our hands. It is a sobering responsibility that merits our consistent attention and care. Any one of us can miss it in the many day-to-day decisions we are each responsible to make. But to consistently overlook foreign-missions giving seriously grieves the heart of God.

I shudder to think of the moment when we will stand before Jesus and give an account for what we did or did not do for those who needed to hear the Gospel message. Those who gave sacrificially will be elated to look into His loving eyes. But those who gave nothing to reach the lost will not stand as pleasingly before the Savior who gave His life to reach them!

DOES IT SEEM THE LAST DAYS ARE GOING ON *FOREVER*?

When the apostle Peter wrote about the last days, he said, "Knowing this first, that there shall come in the last days scoffers, walking after their own lusts, and saying, Where is the promise of his coming?... All things continue as they were from the beginning of the creation" (2 Peter 3:3,4).

In our own time, there are many scoffers who mock those who believe that these are the last days. These cynical "dissenters" argue that people have been talking about "the last days" for 2,000 years, yet nothing has changed during that time. Some even allege that the return of Christ is a fantasy.

The word "scoffers" in Greek means *those who make fun of something through mockery.* This group says, "If Christ was going to come, He would have come by now. The world hasn't really changed that much over the years. We simply have better news coverage, so we're more *aware* of the darkness and tragedy in the world." Many of them are bold to assert that the heralding of

Christ's soon return is based on fictitious prophetic utterances that have no basis in reality — or on ancient texts that are irrelevant to the present day.

Peter predicted the day when scoffers would rise up before Jesus returns and mock people like me — those who preach the message and write books like this one you hold in your hands. And they will mock people like *you* if you believe the time of Christ's return is indeed near.

But what these mockers don't understand is that the last days started on the Day of Pentecost when the Holy Spirit was poured out (*see* Acts 2:16-20). For some 2,000 years, we have been living in what is theologically called the period of *the last days*. That may seem like a long time to us, but Second Peter 3:8 says, "...Beloved, be not ignorant of this one thing, that one day is with the Lord as a thousand years, and a thousand years as one day."

Theologically, this 2,000-year period called "the last days" has only been about two days on God's prophetic calendar! But why has God taken so long to wrap up this period and move to the next prophetic phase? The next verse, Second Peter 3:9, answers that question: "The Lord is not slack concerning His promise, as some count slackness; but is longsuffering to us-ward, not willing that any should perish, but that all should come to repentance."

GOD IS NOT LATE!

The word "slack" is a Greek word that means to be *tardy, slow, delayed,* or *late* in time. By using this word, the Holy Spirit tells us that God is not slow regarding the promises He has made. He made them, and He will fulfill them — but He is "longsuffering" for the sake of those who still need to come to repentance. The end will occur the *instant* the last person who is going to be saved is brought into the Kingdom — and then we will be miraculously transformed and translated to meet the Lord in the air.

The word "longsuffering" is from the Greek word *makrothumia,* a compound of the word *makros* and *thumia,* as we saw in the last chapter. The word *makros* means *long* — and the word *thumia* describes *great patience.* Therefore, this word means to be longsuffering and patient. It is the Holy Spirit who *could* take revenge on a sin-ridden society, but who *utterly refuses* to do so. The delay of God's *punishment* rests on God's *longsuffering.*

God is exceedingly patient with those who are unsaved, and He is willing to wait for the redemption of that *one last person* who will repent. That is the longsuffering of God — and the reason why He has waited, waited, and waited to end this period or age. God is not tardy, delayed, or slow in fulfilling His promise. He is simply holding out for the last soul to be saved.

Second Peter 3:9 states that God is "...not willing that any should perish...." Although it's true that not all will be saved, God is waiting for the Gospel to reach the ends of the earth and for that last person who will respond to His call.

This shows just how *long* the longsuffering of God is! He will wait 2,000 years just for one person to come to

God is not tardy, delayed, or slow in fulfilling His promise. He is simply holding out for the last soul to be saved.

repentance. You see, God knows what hell is, and He doesn't want *anyone* to go there — which is why we *must* be serious and committed about taking the saving message of Jesus to the world in this hour, at the end of this age. We must win as many as possible because that door is still open for the lost to be saved — to be brought into glorious fellowship with God, to avoid hell, and to make Heaven their eternal home.

God's intense desire for the saving of souls should help us better understand this "final" sign of the end of the age. The preaching of the Gospel throughout the entire world will be the very last, *final,* indicator of the last days *just before Jesus comes.*

Think About It

1. Because of the swift development of travel and technology, it is becoming more and more possible naturally to reach the entire world with the Gospel. Describe how this rapid advancement, even in the last 20 years, is a fulfillment of Daniel's last-days prophecy that "...many shall run to and fro, and knowledge shall be increased" (Daniel 12:4).

2. How does the ridicule that Noah endured in his day compare with mockers today who scoff at the notion that Jesus' return is near? Do the striking similarities inspire you to be more earnest in winning souls to Christ?

3. Picture yourself as the believer tasked with the privilege of leading the very last soul to repent just before Jesus returns. Read Second Peter 3:3-10, and consider the great kindness and longsuffering of God as He waits for that last person to be saved!

Chapter Thirteen

How Should We Respond?

In this book, we have looked in-depth at specific signs Jesus gave to alert us that we are nearing the wrap-up of the age. Jesus declared that these signs — like road markers along a highway — should awaken us to the fact that the prophetic road we're on is leading us straight to the time of His return.

Especially in Matthew 24 and Luke 21, we have seen that Jesus forecasted at the very end of the age, there would be an emergence of the following events and trends in society:

- worldwide moral delusion
- doctrinal deception in the Church
- wars and rumors of wars
- political upheavals
- revolutions
- commotions
- uncivil politics
- nations rising against nations

- kingdoms rising against kingdoms

- famines, shortages, and deficits of all types

- great numbers of earthquakes

- the emergence of old and new diseases

- monstrous developments, perhaps in science

- great signs descending from the heavens

- persecution and prosecution of believers

- false prophets and widespread false religious movements

- the increase of iniquity across the face of the earth

- the love of many waxing cold

- the Gospel being heralded to every part of the world as a precursor to the very end of the age

But in addition to the signs Jesus gave that we've already covered extensively in this book, there are additional signs that need to be seriously pondered and discussed.

In Second Timothy 3:1, the apostle Paul prophetically declared, "This know also, that in the last days perilous times shall come." After that, he listed disturbing moral and social developments that will appear in society across the earth at the end of the age. According to Paul, when we see these developments become widespread, they are also to be taken as indicators that the end of the age is upon us.

Few people would question that we are living in dangerous and treacherous times. Regardless of where they live, people have been rudely awakened to the truth that the world is no longer the place it was not so many decades ago.

This present season is far removed from the world many of us remember as children. It is difficult to imagine how things could have spiraled downward so quickly. However, nearly 2,000 years ago when the apostle Paul wrote the book of Second Timothy, the Holy Spirit spoke through him to alert us that such a day *would* come.

⌢⌢

Regardless of where they live, people have been rudely awakened to the truth that the world is no longer the place it was not so many decades ago.

⌢⌢

Paul wrote, "This know also, that in the last times, perilous times shall come" (2 Timothy 3:1). The word "know" in this verse is a translation of the Greek word *ginosko*, a common word that is normally translated *knowledge*. But in this verse, Paul used *ginosko* in the present imperative tense, which means that whatever the Holy Spirit was about to say was so critical that it *must* be recognized, *must* be acknowledged, and *must* be known and understood!

Paul then told us exactly what we MUST know.

He alerted us that in the very last days "perilous times shall come." The word "perilous" comes from the Greek word *chalepos*, a word that it is used only two times in the 27 books of the New Testament. This word was used to denote spoken words that were *hurtful, harsh, cruel, ruthless, cutting, wounding*, and therefore *hard to bear*. But *chalepos* was also used to describe animals that were *vicious, ferocious, fierce, unruly, uncontrollable, unpredictable*, and *dangerous*. In nearly every place where *chalepos* is used in secular literature of the ancient world, it depicts *something said that is harmful*, or it pictures *an environment besieged with high risk or danger*.

Besides Second Timothy 3:1, the only other instance of the word *chalepos* in the New Testament is in Matthew 8:28, where Matthew used it to describe two demon-possessed men. Matthew 8:28 vividly tells us, "And when he [Jesus] was come to the other side into the country of the Gadarenes, there met him two possessed with devils, coming out of the tombs, *exceeding fierce*, so that no man might pass by that way."

The words "exceeding fierce" in Matthew 8:28 are actually a translation of the Greek word *chalepos*. Because *chalepos* is used to describe these two demon-possessed men, it categorically conveys that they were vicious, ferocious, fierce, unruly, uncontrollable, unpredictable, and dangerous.

In fact, if you read the entire account in Matthew's gospel, it's clear that the people who lived in the region of the Gadarenes kept a safe distance between themselves and these two men because they knew that being in close proximity to them would put their lives in jeopardy. These two demon-possessed men were *chalepos* — *vicious, ferocious, fierce, unruly, uncontrollable, unpredictable,* and *dangerous.* But they represented no threat to Jesus because He knew He had authority over the demon spirits that had been granted access to those men's lives. Therefore, instead of running like everyone else, Jesus stood up against those dark forces and set those men free.

This brings us back to Second Timothy 3:1, where the Holy Spirit prophesies through Paul that "perilous times shall come." If you take all the original Greek words into consideration, it delivers a potent message from the Spirit of God: *"You emphatically MUST KNOW what I am about to tell you! In the last days, periods of time will come that are hurtful, harmful, dangerous, unpredictable, uncontrollable, and high-risk...."*

The Holy Spirit graciously warned us 2,000 years ago that the world would become a dangerous place at the end of the age. We just had no idea how fast or how far it would spin out of control. But as we live in the world today, we are waking up to the harsh reality of a rapidly changing society that has become an "exceedingly fierce" place.

Because the word "perilous" (the Greek word *chalepos*) is used to describe the demon-possessed men in Matthew 8:28, I personally believe the Holy Spirit was warning us that demonic activity will be released in the last days that will bring about hurtful, harsh, cruel, ruthless, cutting, and wounding situations that will be emotionally hard to bear. As a result of demonic activity, the world will become a place that is vicious, ferocious, fierce, unruly, uncontrollable, unpredictable, and dangerous. Of course, we know that these forces have access to society through the *people* who give place to them. That is another reason why evangelism and sound preaching and teaching from the Bible is so important.

We are living in a generation that faces threats that no recent generation has ever known. *As always, the Holy Spirit was correct in what He was trying to tell us.*

How should we as believers respond to all of this?

- Should we stay in our houses, close the blinds, and hide from what's going on in the world?

- Should we never fly on a plane again or take public transportation?

- Should we stop frequenting restaurants and other public places — or stop attending large events, such as movies, theatrical productions, and competitions in sports?

- Should we stop sending our children to public schools?

- Should we respond in faith or in fear to these Spirit-predicted truths and the external reality that continually faces us?

Instead of retreating in fear, you and I must accept the challenge to step forward as Jesus did when He encountered the demon-possessed men of the Gadarenes. What terrified other people and made them retreat in fear is exactly what beckoned Jesus to action. *In this hour, we simply must not shrink back!*

The situation in today's world beckons you to action. This is a time for you to step forward and use the authority Jesus Christ gave you to bring deliverance, freedom, and peace to each place that the devil has tried to bring chaos, harm, and hurt. The situation that exists in the world today is your opportunity to let the power and glory of God shine through you!

In the last days of this period, you can learn how to live for Christ victoriously without being affected or scathed by the times in which we live. While society sinks deeper into deception and depravity, God's Word and His Spirit can enable you to rise above the downfall of the world, high above the "waters" of destruction that will cover the earth at the end of the age before Jesus returns for His Church.

The situation that exists in the world today is your opportunity to let the power and glory of God shine through you!

In Second Timothy 3:1-17, Paul warned about key developments that will be seen in society at the culmination of the age. He then instructed us on how to overcome those days if we are living in them.

The following are 17 truths that the apostle wrote regarding what was to come. I enumerated separately each of the verses in this passage in Second Timothy 3 so you could see for yourself the specific developments that will occur and that are, in fact, occurring now. The last verses tell us how to prepare for these times in order to live victoriously and be a powerful witness for Christ.

1. **This know also, that in the last days perilous times shall come.**

2. For men shall be lovers of their own selves, covetous, boasters, proud, blasphemers, disobedient to parents, unthankful, unholy,

3. Without natural affection, trucebreakers, false accusers, incontinent, fierce, despisers of those that are good,

4. Traitors, heady, highminded, lovers of pleasures more than lovers of God;

5. Having a form of godliness, but denying the power thereof: from such turn away.

6. For of this sort are they which creep into houses, and lead captive silly women laden with sins, led away with divers lusts,

7. Ever learning, and never able to come to the knowledge of the truth.

8. Now as Jannes and Jambres withstood Moses, so do these also resist the truth: men of corrupt minds, reprobate concerning the faith.

9. But they shall proceed no further: for their folly shall be manifest unto all men, as theirs also was.

10. But thou hast fully known my doctrine, manner of life, purpose, faith, longsuffering, charity, patience,

11. Persecutions, afflictions, which came unto me at Antioch, at Iconium, at Lystra; what persecutions I endured: but out of them all the Lord delivered me.

12. Yea, and all that will live godly in Christ Jesus shall suffer persecution.

13. But evil men and seducers shall wax worse and worse, deceiving, and being deceived.

14. But continue thou in the things which thou hast learned and hast been assured of, knowing of whom thou hast learned them;

15. **And that from a child thou hast known the holy scriptures** [writing specifically to Timothy], **which are able to make thee** [this applies to every one of us] **wise unto salvation through faith which is in Christ Jesus.**

16. **All scripture is given by inspiration of God, and is profitable for doctrine, for reproof, for correction, for instruction in righteousness:**

17. **That the man of God may be perfect, thoroughly furnished unto all good works.**

Paul was painting a prophetic picture to every believer concerning future times and seasons. But this "picture" *especially* applies to those who will be living in the season of Christ's return and the rapture of the Church. Nevertheless, this passage provides admonition and instruction that every believer of all time is called upon to embrace and take into his or her heart.

Although the world is sinking deeper into fear and darkness, this is our best hour as children of God. Rather than succumb to fear, it's time for you to tell fear to *leave* you in Jesus' name! Then along the prophetic road, embrace the opportunities you encounter to bring deliverance and freedom to people gripped with this demonic stronghold by the news they hear each day.

Think of it. God has called you — and has empowered you with His Word and His Spirit — to live victoriously for Him and to fulfill His purpose for your life in these last of the last days! So embrace the honor of being in His plan. Determine to trust Him with your life — to be who He needs you to be in every moment of this prophetic season!

YOU ARE CALLED AND ANOINTED

In this book, we've looked at signs Jesus said we would witness in the very last days before His imminent return. The signs are occurring closer and closer as we draw nearer to the conclusion of this age. Like the birth pains a woman feels when she is in labor, it seems the breathing space between each event is getting shorter and shorter.

I urge you to ask the Holy Spirit to open your heart and mind and to show you how you should respond to the information and truths contained in this book. Jesus prophesied it all with pinpoint accuracy. He did not speak these things to scare us, but rather to help prepare us so we could dodge the spiritual landmines that lie scattered over an end-times landscape.

The Holy Spirit wants to help you navigate *victoriously* the last "minutes and seconds" of the age. I advise you to dig deep into the Scriptures, stick with time-tested truth, regardless of trends in society, and allow the Holy Spirit to fill you with the power you need to overcome every obstacle. *You are called and anointed for this end-times season!* So embrace that truth and charge forward in the power of the Spirit to shine the light of God's Word into an ever-darkening world.

Think About It

1. Comparing this last-days season to a scoreboard's *last* minutes and seconds in the *last* quarter of a football game, what is your best understanding of your role in this great "end-times game"?

2. *Every* believer will respond in some way to the events of a last-days society. To make no response is a response nonetheless! Which of the following ways best describes how you're participating in an end-times culture? Are you: a) blending in with society, accepting "revised morality" as normal? b) riding the fence to avoid persecution and rejection? c) holding fast to the truth in the face of opposition so you can experience God's power? If you're not satisfied with your honest answer, it's not too late to make adjustments that will please God and count for all eternity.

PRAYER OF SALVATION

When Jesus Christ comes into your life, you are immediately emancipated — totally set free from the bondage of sin! If you have never received Jesus as your personal Savior, it is time to experience this new life for yourself. The first step to freedom is simple. Just pray this prayer from your heart:

Lord, I can never adequately thank You for all You did for me on the Cross. I am so undeserving, Jesus, but You came and gave Your life for me anyway. I repent for rejecting You, and I turn away from my life of rebellion and sin right now. I turn to You and receive You as my Savior, and I ask You to wash away my sin and make me completely new in You by Your precious blood. I thank You from the depths of my heart for doing what no one else could do for me. Had it not been for Your willingness to lay down Your life for me, I would be eternally lost.

Thank You, Jesus, that I am now redeemed by Your blood. On the Cross, You bore my sin, my sickness, my pain, my lack of peace, and my suffering. Your blood has removed my sin, washed me whiter than snow, and given me rightstanding with the Father. I have no need to be ashamed of my past sins because I am now a new creature in You. Old things have passed away, and all things have become new because I am in Jesus Christ (2 Corinthians 5:17).

Because of You, Jesus, today I am forgiven; I am filled with peace; and I am a joint-heir with You! Satan no longer has a right to lay any claim on me. From a grateful heart, I will faithfully serve You the rest of my days!

If you prayed this prayer from your heart, something amazing has happened to you. No longer a servant to sin, you are now a servant of Almighty God. The evil spirits that once exacted every ounce of your being and required your all-inclusive servitude no longer possess the authorization to control you or dictate your destiny!

As a result of your decision to turn your life over to Jesus Christ, your eternal home has been decided forever. Heaven will now be your permanent address for all eternity.

God's Spirit has moved into your own human spirit, and you have become the "temple of God" (1 Corinthians 6:19). What a miracle! To think that God, by His Spirit, now lives inside you!

Now you have a new Lord and Master, and His name is Jesus. From this moment on, the Spirit of God will work in you and supernaturally energize you to fulfill God's will for your life. Everything will change for you as you yield to His leadership in your life — and it's all going to change for the best!

ENDNOTES

Chapter 4

[1]Milton Leitenberg, "Deaths in Wars and Conflicts in the 20th Century, 3rd ed." (2006) Cornell University Peace Studies Program, Occasional Paper #29.

[2]"Global Terrorism Index." (2016) Institute for Economics and Peace. http://economicsandpeace.org/wp-content/uploads/2016/11/Global-Terrorism-Index-2016.2.pdf

Chapter 5

[1]Jean-Marie Guehenno, "Ten Wars To Watch in 2015." (Jan. 2, 2015). Foreign Policy Magazine. https://foreignpolicy.com/2015/01/02/10-wars-to-watch-in-2015

Chapter 6

[1]"2016 World Hunger and Poverty Facts and Statistics." (2016) World Hunger Education Service. https://www.worldhunger.org/2015-world-hunger-and-poverty-facts-and-statistics

[2]"2016 World Hunger and Poverty Facts and Statistics." (2016) World Hunger Education Service. https://www.worldhunger.org/2015-world-hunger-and-poverty-facts-and-statistics

[3]"How Close Are We to Zero Hunger?: The State of Food Security in the World." (2017) Food and Agriculture Administration of the United Nations. http://www.fao.org/state-of-food-security-nutrition/en

[4]"How Close Are We to Zero Hunger?: The State of Food Security in the World." (2017) Food and Agriculture Administration of the United Nations. http://www.fao.org/state-of-food-security-nutrition/en

[5]"2016 World Hunger and Poverty Facts and Statistics." (2016) World Hunger Education Service. https://www.worldhunger.org/2015-world-hunger-and-poverty-facts-and-statistics

[6]"How Close Are We to Zero Hunger?: The State of Food Security in the World." (2017) Food and Agriculture Administration of the United Nations. http://www.fao.org/state-of-food-security-nutrition/en

[7] "World Development Indicators 2013." Washington, D.C.: World Bank. http://data.worldbank.org/data-catalog/world-development-indicators

Chapter 7

[1]Sofia Zyga, "Emerging and Re-emerging Infectious Diseases: A Potential Pandemic Threat" (2011) Health Science Journal 5.3.

[2]"2014 Ebola Outbreak in West Africa — Case Counts." (Apr. 13, 2016). Centers for Disease Control. https://www.cdc.gov/vhf/ebola/outbreaks/2014-west-africa/case-counts.html

[3]Pim Martens and Maud Huynen, "A Future Without Health? Health Dimension in Global Scenario Studies," Bulletin of the World Health Organization 2003, 81 (12).

[4]"Emerging Diseases." World Health Organization. http://www.searo.who.int/topics/emerging_diseases/en

[5]Pim Martens and Maud Huynen, "A Future Without Health? Health Dimension in Global Scenario Studies," Bulletin of the World Health Organization 2003, 81 (12).

[6]K. F. Smith, M. Goldberg, S. Rosenthal, L. Carlson, J. Chen, C. Chen, and S. Ramachandran, "Global Rise in Human Infectious Disease Outbreaks," Journal of the Royal Society Interface. (Oct. 2014). https://doi.org/10.1098/rsif.2014.0950

[7]Ole Benedictow, "The Black Death: The Greatest Catastrophe Ever." (2005) History Today, Volume 55. Issue 3. http://www.historytoday.com/ole-j-benedictow/black-death-greatest-catastrophe-ever

[8]"HIV/AID: Global Health Observatory Data." (2017) WHO. http://www.who.int/mediacentre/factsheets/fs360/en

[9]"HIV/AIDS 101: Global Statistics." (Nov. 29, 2016). https://www.hiv.gov/hiv-basics/overview/data-and-trends/global-statistics

[10]"HIV/AIDS: Key Facts." (Feb. 15, 2018). WHO. http://www.who.int/mediacentre/factsheets/fs360/en

[11]Christian Nordqvist, "HIV/AIDS Causes, Symptoms and Treatments." (May 11, 2016). Medical News Today. http://www.medicalnewstoday.com/articles/17131.php

[12]"HIV/AIDS: Fact Sheet." (Nov. 2016). WHO. http://www.who.int/mediacentre/factsheets/fs360/en

[13]"Global Fact Sheet." (2012) UNAIDS. http://files.unaids.org/en/media/unaids/contentassets/documents/epidemiology/2012/gr2012/20121120_FactSheet_Global_en.pdf

[14]"Children AIDS: 2015 Statistical Update." (2015) UNICEF. https://reliefweb.int/sites/reliefweb.int/files/resources/executive_summary_digital.pdf

[15]"HIV/AIDS: Fact Sheet." (Nov. 2016). WHO. http://www.who.int/en/news-room/fact-sheets/detail/hiv-aids

[16]"CDC Fact Sheet." (2016) Center for Disease Control. https://www.cdc.gov/nchhstp/newsroom/docs/factsheets/todaysepidemic-508.pdf

[17]"HIV/AIDS." (Feb. 2018). WHO. http://www.who.int/mediacentre/factsheets/fs360/en

[18]"Estimated Incidence and Prevalence in the United States 2010-2015," HIV Surveillance Supplemental Report (2018);23(1). CDC. https://www.cdc.gov/hiv/group/age/youth/index.html

[19]"HIV/AIDS." (Nov. 2017). WHO. http://www.who.int/features/qa/71/en

[20]Brandon S. Razooky, et al., "A Hardwired HIV Latency Program," Cell 160.5 (2015), pp. 990-1001.

[21]"HIV Among Youth." (Apr. 27, 2016). CDC. https://www.cdc.gov/hiv/group/age/youth

[22]"HIV/AIDS 101: U.S. Statistics." (Nov. 29, 2016). CDC. https://www.hiv.gov/hiv-basics/overview/data-and-trends/global-statistics

[23]"HIV Among Gay and Bisexual Men." (Feb. 27, 2018). CDC. https://www.cdc.gov/hiv/group/msm/index.html

Chapter 8

[1]T. Lay, H. Kanamori, C. J. Ammon, M. Nettles, S. N. Ward, R. C. Aster, S. L. Beck, S. L. Bilek, M. R. Brudzinski, R. Butler, and H. R.

DeShon, "The Great Sumatra-Andaman Earthquake of 26 December 2004," Science 308(5725) (2015), pp.1127-1133.

[2]"2004 Indian Ocean Earthquake." (April 27, 2018). New World Encyclopedia. http://www.newworldencyclopedia.org/p/index.php?title=2004_Indian_Ocean_earthquake&oldid=1011144

[3]About Us: Program Overview. United States Geological Survey. https://earthquake.usgs.gov/aboutus

[4]"Why Are We Having So Many Earthquakes?...." https://www.usgs.gov/faqs/why-are-we-having-so-many-earthquakes-has-naturally-occurring-earthquake-activity-been?qt-news_science_products=0#qt-news_science_products

[5]Peter M. Shearer and Philip B. Stark, "Global Risk of Big Earthquakes Has Not Recently Increased," Proceedings of the National Academy of Sciences 109.3 (2012), pp. 717-721.

[6]"How Often Do Earthquakes Occur?" (June 2011). Education and Outreach Series No. 3. Incorporated Research Institutions for Seismology. https://www.iris.edu/hq/files/publications/brochures_onepagers/doc/EN_OnePager3.pdf

[7]"Frequency of Earthquakes Worldwide: Table." National Earthquake Information Center, USGS. https://www.infoplease.com/world/earthquakes/frequency-earthquakes-worldwide

[8]"Earthquake Facts." USGS. https://earthquake.usgs.gov/learn/facts.php

Chapter 9

[1]"Where Does Christian Persecution Occur?" Open Doors. https://www.opendoorsusa.org/christian-persecution/where-does-christian-persecution-occur

[2]"World Watch List 2018: The 50 Countries Where It's Most Dangerous To Follow Jesus." (2018) Open Doors. https://www.opendoorsusa.org/wp-content/uploads/2017/05/WWL2018-Booklet-11518.pdf

[3]"Christian Persecution." (2017) Open Doors. https://www.opendoorsusa.org/christian-persecution/world-watch-list

[4]"Where Does Christian Persecution Occur?" Open Doors. https://www.opendoorsusa.org/christian-persecution/where-does-christian-persecution-occur

[5]"Christian Persecution." (2017) Open Doors. https://www.opendoorsusa.org/christian-persecution/world-watch-list

[6]"World Watch List 2018: The 50 Countries Where It's Most Dangerous To Follow Jesus." (2018) Open Doors. https://www.opendoorsusa.org/wp-content/uploads/2017/05/WWL2018-Booklet-11518.pdf

[7]"Why Persecution Occurs?" (2017) Open Doors. https://www.opendoorsusa.org/christian-persecution/why-persecution-occurs

[8]Samuel Smith, "2015 Deadliest Year for Christians, Open Doors' World Watch List Finds." (Jan. 13, 2016). The Christian Post. http://www.christianpost.com/news/open-doors-world-watch-list-2015-deadliest-year-christians-killed-for-faith-jesus-christ-154875

[9]"Christian Persecution." (2018) Open Doors. https://www.opendoorsusa.org/christian-persecution/world-watch-list

[10]"World Watch List 2018: The 50 Countries Where It's Most Dangerous To Follow Jesus." (2018) Open Doors. https://www.opendoorsusa.org/wp-content/uploads/2017/05/WWL2018-Booklet-11518.pdf

[11]"Religious Freedom in the World Report Executive Summary 2016." ACN International. http://religion-freedom-report.org.uk/wp-content/uploads/2016/11/Religious-Freedom-in-the-World-Executive-Summary-2016.pdf

[12]Stoyan Zaimov, "Over 100 Million Christians Are Being Persecuted for Their Faith in Jesus Christ, Says Christian Charity Report." (July 31, 2015). The Christian Post. https://www.christianpost.com/news/over-100-million-christians-are-being-persecuted-for-their-faith-in-jesus-christ-says-christian-charity-report-142144

[13]"North Korea." Christian Solidarity Worldwide. http://www.csw.org.uk/our_work_profile_northkorea.htm

Chapter 10

[1]"Who Was Edgar Cayce?" Edgar Cayce's A.R.E. https://www.edgarcayce.org/edgar-cayce/his-life

[2]"Unification Church." (Oct. 28, 2016). Religion Facts. http://www.religionfacts.com/unification-church

[3]"New Age." (Oct. 28, 2016). Religion Facts. http://www.religionfacts.com/new-age

Chapter 12

[1]Rick Renner, "What Happened to the Other Apostles?" *A Light in Darkness, Volume One* (Tulsa, OK: Harrison House 2010, 2018), pp. 48-55.

[2]"Joshua Group: Global Statistics." (2017) Joshua Project. https://joshua project.net/people_groups/statistics

[3]"Mobile Phone Users Worldwide 2013-2019." (2017) Statista. https://www.statista.com/statistics/274774/forecast-of-mobile-phone-users -worldwide

[4]"World Population Prospects: The 2017 Revision." (Jun. 21, 2017). United Nations Department of Economic and Social Affairs. https://www.un.org/development/desa/publications/world-population-prospects -the-2017-revision.html

[5]Ethnologue: Languages of the World. https://www.ethnologue.com/browse/families

[6]"Number of TV Households Worldwide From 2010 to 2021 (in Billions)" (2018) Statista. https://www.statista.com/statistics/268695/number-of-tv-households-worldwide

ABOUT THE AUTHOR

 **Rick Renner** is a highly respected Bible teacher and leader in the international Christian community. Rick is the author of the bestsellers *Dressed To Kill* and *Sparkling Gems From the Greek, 1* and *2*, which have sold more than 3 million copies combined.

Rick is also the founder and president of Rick Renner Ministries, based in Tulsa, Oklahoma, and host to his TV program that is seen around the world in multiple languages. Rick leads this amazing work with his wife and lifelong ministry partner, Denise, along with the help of their sons and committed leadership team.

REFERENCE BOOK LIST

1. *How To Use New Testament Greek Study Aids* by Walter Jerry Clark (Loizeaux Brothers).

2. *Strong's Exhaustive Concordance of the Bible* by James H. Strong.

3. *The Interlinear Greek-English New Testament* by George Ricker Berry (Baker Book House).

4. *The Englishman's Greek Concordance of the New Testament* by George Wigram (Hendrickson).

5. *New Thayer's Greek-English Lexicon of the New Testament* by Joseph Thayer (Hendrickson).

6. *The Expanded Vine's Expository Dictionary of New Testament Words* by W. E. Vine (Bethany).

7. *New International Dictionary of New Testament Theology* (*DNTT*); Colin Brown, editor (Zondervan).

8. *Theological Dictionary of the New Testament* (*TDNT*) by Geoffrey Bromiley; Gephard Kittle, editor (Eerdmans Publishing Co.).

9. *The New Analytical Greek Lexicon*; Wesley Perschbacher, editor (Hendrickson).

10. *The Linguistic Key to the Greek New Testament* by Fritz Rienecker and Cleon Rogers (Zondervan).

11. *Word Studies in the Greek New Testament* by Kenneth Wuest, 4 Volumes (Eerdmans).

12. *New Testament Words* by William Barclay (Westminster Press).

CONTACT RENNER MINISTRIES

For further information
about RENNER Ministries, please contact
the RENNER Ministries office nearest you,
or visit the ministry website at
www.renner.org.

**ALL USA
CORRESPONDENCE:**
RENNER Ministries
P. O. Box 702040
Tulsa, OK 74170-2040
(918) 496-3213
Or 1-800-RICK-593
Email: renner@renner.org
Website: www.renner.org

MOSCOW OFFICE:
RENNER Ministries
P. O. Box 789
Moscow 101000, Russia
+7 (495) 727-14-67
Email: partner@rickrenner.ru
Website: www.ignc.org

RIGA OFFICE:
RENNER Ministries
Unijas 99
Riga LV-1084, Latvia
+(371) 67802150
Email: info@goodnews.lv

KIEV OFFICE:
RENNER Ministries
P. O. Box 300
01001, Ukraine, Kiev
+38 (044) 451-8115
Email: partner@rickrenner.ru

OXFORD OFFICE:
RENNER Ministries
Box 7, 266 Banbury Road
Oxford OX2 7DL, England 44
+44 (0) 1865 355509
Email: europe@renner.org

DRESSED TO KILL — A BIBLICAL APPROACH TO SPIRITUAL WARFARE AND ARMOR

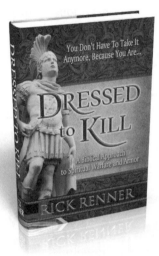

$24.97 (Hardback)

Rick Renner's book ***Dressed To Kill*** is considered by many to be a true classic on the subject of spiritual warfare. The original version, which sold more than 400,000 copies, is a curriculum staple in Bible schools worldwide. In this beautifully bound hardback volume, you will find:

- 512 pages of reedited text

- 16 pages of full-color illustrations

- Questions at the end of each chapter to guide you into deeper study

In ***Dressed To Kill***, Rick explains with exacting detail the purpose and function of each piece of Roman armor. In the process, he describes the significance of our *spiritual* armor not only to withstand the onslaughts of the enemy, but also to overturn the tendencies of the carnal mind. Furthermore, Rick delivers a clear, scriptural presentation on the biblical definition of spiritual warfare — what it is and what it is not.

When you walk with God in deliberate, continual fellowship, He will enrobe you with Himself. Armed with the knowledge of who you are in Him, you will be dressed and dangerous to the works of darkness, unflinching in the face of conflict, and fully equipped to take the offensive and gain mastery over any opposition from your spiritual foe. You don't have to accept defeat anymore once you are *dressed to kill*!

To order, visit us online at: **www.renner.org**

Book Resellers: Contact Harrison House at 800-888-4126 or visit **www.HarrisonHouse.com** for quantity discounts.

SPARKLING GEMS FROM THE GREEK 1

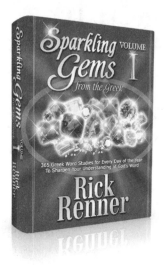

In 2003, Rick Renner's *Sparkling Gems From the Greek 1* quickly gained widespread recognition for its unique illumination of the New Testament through more than 1,000 Greek word studies in a 365-day devotional format. Today *Sparkling Gems 1* remains a beloved resource that has spiritually strengthened believers worldwide. As many have testified, the wealth of truths within its pages never grows old. Year after year, *Sparkling Gems 1* continues to deepen readers' understanding of the Bible.

$34.97 (Hardback)
1,048 pages

To order, visit us online at: **www.renner.org**

SPARKLING GEMS FROM THE GREEK 2

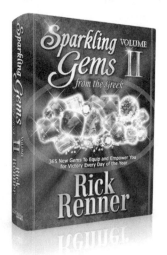

Now Rick infuses into *Sparkling Gems From the Greek 2* the added strength and richness of many more years of his own personal study and growth in God — expanding this devotional series to impact the reader's heart on a deeper level than ever before. This remarkable study tool helps unlock new hidden treasures from God's Word that will draw readers into an ever more passionate pursuit of Him.

$49.97 (Hardback)
1,280 pages

To order, visit us online at: **www.renner.org**

LIFE IN THE COMBAT ZONE

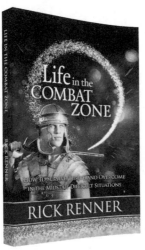

The battle lines are drawn. A collision course is set. In the coming battle, will you rush the front lines or shrink from the conflict? Although the risk is great, the rewards for remaining in the fight are sure.

In *Life in the Combat Zone*, Rick Renner encourages you to *fight* like a Roman soldier, *train* like a Greek athlete, and *work* like a farmer — all to become that unwavering warrior who hears God's voice, surrenders to His call, and willingly enters the combat zone poised to win.

Spiritual conflicts are real and unavoidable. There are no shortcuts to victory, but there *can* be an inevitable outcome. Rick will help you discover the key qualities you'll need to withstand the heat of the battle so you can emerge triumphant and receive the victor's crown.

$17.00 (Paperback)
272 pages

To order, visit us online at: **www.renner.org**

Book Resellers: Contact Harrison House at 800-888-4126 or visit **www.HarrisonHouse.com** for quantity discounts.

BOOKS BY RICK RENNER

Dream Thieves*
Dressed To Kill*
The Holy Spirit and You!* (formerly titled, *The Dynamic Duo*)
How To Receive Answers From Heaven!*
Insights to Successful Leadership
Life in the Combat Zone*
A Light in Darkness, Volume One
The Love Test*
No Room for Compromise, A Light in Darkness, Volume Two
Paid in Full*
The Point of No Return*
Repentance*
Say Yes!* (formerly titled, *If You Were God, Would You Choose You?*)
Seducing Spirits and Doctrines of Demons
Signs You'll See Just Before Jesus Comes
Sparkling Gems From the Greek
   Daily Devotional 1*
Sparkling Gems From the Greek
   Daily Devotional 2*
Spiritual Weapons To Defeat the Enemy*
Ten Guidelines To Help You Achieve
   Your Long-Awaited Promotion!*
365 Days of Power*
Turn Your God-Given Dreams Into Reality*
Why We Need the Gifts of the Spirit*
You Can Get Over It*

*Digital version available for Kindle, Nook, iBook,
and other eBook formats.
Note: Books by Rick Renner are available for purchase at:
www.renner.org

The Harrison House Vision

Proclaiming the truth and the power

of the Gospel of Jesus Christ with excellence.

Challenging Christians

to live victoriously,

grow spiritually,

know God intimately.

Connect with us on
Facebook @ HarrisonHousePublishers
and Instagram @ HarrisonHousePublishing
so you can stay up to date with news
about our books and our authors.

Visit us at **www.harrisonhouse.com**
for a complete product listing as well as
monthly specials for wholesale distribution.

Notes

Notes

Notes

_____
_____
_____
_____
_____
_____
_____
_____
_____
_____
_____
_____
_____
_____
_____
_____
_____
_____
_____
_____

Notes

Notes

Notes

Notes

Notes

Notes

Notes

Notes

Notes

Notes